ENDURING LOVE

Venessa Marie Perry

ISBN: 0692798501
ISBN 13: 9780692798508
Library of Congress Control Number: 2016917611
VMP Media, New York, NY

INTRODUCTION

L ove. We all need it, seek it, suffer from the lack of it and have a hard time defining what we mean by the word. Parents love their children, and children want that love to be unconditional. We love our siblings one way, our friends another way. If we are fortunate, we love and are loved by many people whose relationship with us is specific to the role we play in one another's lives. We hope and expect to find an ideal love that brings us romance and passion, an adult relationship that begins with partnership and culminates with becoming the beloved's spouse.

And throughout life we find ourselves in relationships that bring trials and tribulations that test the boundaries of love. The personal stories in this book examine the role each woman's experience of spirituality and religious faith played when they faced challenges, defeats, and triumphs as the boundaries of love were tested. In their willingness to share their stories these women exercise personal courage that sheds light on the complex dynamics of love, spirituality and the intersection of the two.

Many women feel that their struggles to live life in accordance with God's plan for them are unique to them; surely, they think, other women find this work easier. But the fundamental questions about love and relationships and the demands of spiritual life provide a common bond between women and across spiritual communities. Women share a strong sense of love's demands. Perhaps the intensity of this feeling is what causes the uncertainty, shame, and embarrassment that so often accompany being a woman of faith longing for romantic, sexual love.

Historically women have been encouraged not to "talk about it" in public, so their worries and longing were only talked about in whispers, behind closed doors, out of ear shot of the rest of the world. Despite all the retreats and classes offered to help women of faith find and maintain exclusive and permanent relationships, in everyday life the topics of love and sexuality are still very taboo in many religious sects and family settings.

The women who confronted these taboos to tell their stories in this book are courageous and inspiring. For some of the women, telling their stories has been cathartic, but still difficult; where necessary, their names have been altered. Through the generously shared personal accounts in this collection, other women will be encouraged to seek out their own understanding of what it means to be a woman of faith – and what it means to love.

<u>Alphabetic by Author</u>

LONELY THE HEART THAT ISN'T FREE
BY MARY DYER HUBBARD

N o one thinks to hug a nun. They seem so untouchable or at least, they did in 1966 when I entered the convent at the age of 18. Every day we new recruits or *postulants* had a study session in which we learned how to be nuns and I was determined to be like Audrey Hepburn in *The Nun's Story* which I had seen with my girlfriends at Radio City Music Hall a few weeks before I got me to a nunnery.

Those first days in the cloister were like a game, trying to remember the minutia of rules: Silence Days are Mondays, Tuesdays, Thursdays and Fridays; never talk in the dormitories or Bathrooms – and certainly not during the Grand Silence from 9:00pm until after prayer, Mass and breakfast in the morning. *Don't wash your hair in the hopper* which I would never think of do- ing until I learned that "hopper" wasn't a toilet but a large sink for washing out mops. *Use the designated receptacle for specials* which I would do if I knew what "specials" were. Turns out they were used sanitary napkins. However the guideline in *The Postulants Manual* that became my undoing was: *Do not touch another person.* It was so contrary to how I was raised.

I grew up in a cookie-cutter split level house in a working class neighborhood of South Jersey. There were ten of us living there: my parents, seven of us kids and my widowed paternal Irish grandmother who called her son one day on the phone and announced, *Charles, I'm coming to live with you.* My Dad scrambled to transform our attached garage into a mini-apartment for her because there were just no more bedrooms. He had already converted the downstairs recreation room into a bedroom for my three brothers with bunk beds and a crib while we four girls had the two upstairs bedrooms. Kathy and I shared the same bed ever since she was one and I was three. My first night in the convent was the first time I ever remember sleeping alone.

My mother's story about how I was named Mary helps understand why I became a nun: *I was seven months pregnant with you and I really wanted a girl after having two boys. I was ironing when I got this idea to pray to the Blessed Mother so I put down the iron and got on my knees. I told her if she would ask God to send me a little girl, I would name her Mary in her honor. When I got up from my knees and turned on the radio there was a crooner singing: "Mary Lou, I love you!" But the Blessed Mother didn't know when to stop! After you, she sent me Kathy, Jeanne and Peggy. It was only when Jimmy came along that she ended her run on girls.* When I was young, I was fascinated listening to this story again and again, feeling both chosen and special. But when I became a teenager, the feeling of being chosen began to tighten uncomfortably around me. Did being chosen mean I didn't have a choice except to be a virgin like Mary?

Our household had some lively times and I loved it there. We always ate meals together at our cramped kitchen table with everyone jostling to be heard. Mom's background as an elementary school teacher came to the fore as she made sure each of us had our few minutes of air time, *Everybody, be quiet. It's Jeanne's turn to talk* and the rest of us would groan to have to listen to her First Grade escapades. Dad, a school administrator, was a quiet serious man who sat at the head of the table while all this cacophony was going on in front of him. We older kids tried to get him to smile, and so told outrageous stories which were rewarded when we spied a tiny twitch at the corner of his mouth.

After supper, we'd all troop into the living room, kneel down in front of the Sacred Heart picture and say our family prayer in which each person had a designated part. This was okay with us kids because we were used to it, but we dreaded May and October when we had to pray the whole rosary together on our knees in honor of the Blessed Mother. During Advent, Mom made an Advent wreath which we lit at suppertime, and on Christmas Day we seven kids performed for our elderly relatives a Christmas play that Mom both wrote and directed. Dad was the main stage hand who handled the curtain, a.k.a. bamboo rod with blanket over it. The tableau scene always brought tears to the eyes of the audience with oldest brother Jack being the narrator, Peter Joseph portraying his namesake, and my younger sisters filling in as shepherds, angels or animals as needed. I of course was typecast as the Blessed Mother and whoever was the youngest kid at the time would be the Baby Jesus, until the year Toddler Peggy gathered up her swaddling clothes and leaped out of the manger saying, "I'm not doing this anymore!"

So that darn rule in *The Postulants Manual* about not touching another person kept haunting me. We were instructed to have *religious decorum*, a somber, dignified way of holding oneself. When we walked, we were to keep *custody of the eyes*, looking down humbly and not having eye-contact with another. *Recreation* was the term for our afternoon exercise, a line of adolescent girls, walking two by two and clad all in black, winding their way quietly through nearby neighborhoods. We were cautioned not to *recreate* with the same postulant again until we'd walked once with every other person in the group. This was to prevent *particular friendships* from forming which confused me greatly since I had many close friends back home, especially my younger sister Kathy, and they were quite dear to me. I didn't realize until years later that many of these stipulations were to prevent homosexual behavior. At that point in my life as a teenager, I didn't even know what that was.

When you live this way, you stiffen. You become wary and distant, lose your spontaneity and pull back in alarm if you inadvertently bump into someone. Yet the rule book said this was a necessary step toward becoming a nun.

An incident one evening stands out in my mind as a terrible consequence of that proscription against touching. There were five of us nuns in training standing together in a small kitchenette before the Grand Silence began. Our Postulant Director came into our midst and told one young woman she'd just received word her father died. That girl was standing right next to me. All I had to do was reach out and put my arm around her in a moment of caring before she left to go to the phone. But I froze. I remember thinking my touch would hurt her: sharp and bony. I kept the rule and I loathed myself for it. Later that night, I heard whispers and soft crying as one of my fellow postulants sat at the top of the stairwell, her arm across the shoulders of our grieving *band mate,* offering soothing words of comfort during the Grand Silence. Eventually both of those young women left the convent, probably because they were deemed too *secular.* But I stayed on and honed my rigidity.

It wasn't until I became a teacher and was sent out to *the missions* that small cracks developed in my armor. Early in my career, I was assigned to teach a self-contained 8th grade class in inner-city New Orleans. As instructed by my elementary education professors, I strove *not to smile before Christmas* which fit in well with my standoffish demeanor. But in my anxiety on that first day of class, I ran through my entire lesson plan in the first 45 minutes of the day. Panicking, I fled to my desk and frantically searched for something else to teach to keep those 33 students from erupting into chaos. Then sweet Ramona came up and placed a gentle hand on my arm, *Sister, could you help me with this problem?* She was touching me, not removing her hand, and I didn't repulse her. A sliver of inner ice began to melt.

Then there was the infamous 7th grade class of 1977 which had run several teachers out of town and maybe out of teaching, I was told before I even met them. Each kid in the class had an animal persona: *ape, horse, woodchuck, frog, duck, etc.* Whenever anyone said a word that rhymed with their designated name, those students were to imitate their appropriate animal sound. It was my misfortune early in my time with them to quote Harry Truman during history class: *The buck stops here.* Of course, the kid who was Duck and the one who was Chuck had to start their quacks and snorts while my back was to them as I wrote on the blackboard. I turned around swiftly, ready with my sternest face to glare them into silence. But all I could think of was us crazy Dyer siblings at the supper table trying to get Dad to snicker and I just burst out laughing.

Those kids were mine from that moment on. I taught them math as if we were on a TV game show, and made English grammar, that vile subject, great fun by having them learn the parts of speech in syncopated chant with some of the boys providing drum beats on their desks while the girls added cheerleading moves. We'd even run through nouns to gerunds on the school bus riding to basketball games.

On the weekends and in the summer, I visited the homes and families of my students whether in New Orleans housing projects or in rural Louisiana or along the bayou. That's when I most felt the old me coming back as Moms called out from their kitchens, *Come on in and don't even knock. Help yourself to whatever's in the refrigerator 'cause you're family here.* And if a baby was in the house?

Everyone knew to bring that child to me as soon as I walked in the door! This helped assuage the ache I felt in not being able to hold and play with my own youngest brother and sister. Jimmy was 4 when I left home and Peggy 7. Now I saw my family only two weeks a year each August, and my younger siblings were growing up without my really knowing them.

As much as my students and their families invited me to be real and touchable, convent life reinforced the old lessons of reserve. At the age of twenty-eight I was one of twelve nuns who sat in our formal convent dining room each day with our impeccable table manners. We wore our religious habits and veils inside the convent as well as out, and we called each other *Sister*. Every month we had a community meeting in which our faults were named in the presence of all the Sisters; we were expected to apologize and correct these immediately. Sister Jane and I, the two youngest in the house, were reprimanded for our lack of religious decorum: we had been seen riding bicycles while visiting families in town. No more. One nun in the house (God bless her) somehow reached mid-life with her humor and sense of self intact. When criticized for some picayune flaw, she'd answer sincerely, *But this is when I'm really trying. You should see me when I'm not!* Lacking decorum, I loved it.

Loneliness became my frequent companion. Gone were those early years in religious life when I felt God's love encompassing me even in the silence and isolation of the cloister. On one particular Saturday morning preparing the next week's lessons in my empty classroom, I found this aloneness crushing. I tried to concentrate on my work but the aching feeling of being cut-off from God, my family and friends, and my own self felt like a trapped animal pawing at me from the inside. I put my head down on a desk and wept. A few minutes later the principal entered, one of the Sisters I lived with. She looked at me with concern and asked, *Sister, what's wrong?* Amazingly, I told her *I'm just so lonely.* She stood there holding my gaze for several moments before turning and quietly leaving the room. We never spoke of this again.

By 1982 when I was thirty-two, my teaching days were over. I was chosen to be the congregation's *Vocation Director,* PR Person, Recruiter. I was to travel the U.S. and find all the young women eager to be nuns, and snatch them up before any other congregations could get to them. It seemed no one realized women were fleeing the convent by then, not clamoring to get into it. During that terrible three year job, I never slept in the same bed more than 16 days in a row and everywhere I went, I disappointed the Sisters. *How many new Postulants will be joining us this year?* Failure now joined loneliness as my twin companions. In the midst of those futile days, I made a retreat at a spirituality center along a tree-lined river in Maryland. It did not lift my spirits. Adding to my negativity was a quirky Jesuit priest who was assigned as retreat director for me and a handful of other nuns for the week. He seemed to ignore the expected routine of selecting Bible verses for meditation, and instead got very New Age-y.

Go outside and let something in nature speak to you. I'll meet you back here after lunch and you can share your discoveries. I walked out angry and rebellious while my group mates scurried about, obediently searching for some personal revelation. One by one, they headed back with an object held reverently in their hands: a flower, a stone, a twig, a leaf. Me? I had nothing. *One more failure to add to my trove,* I thought miserably and wondered if they'd still feed me if I came back empty-handed.

Then something caught my eye. Wasn't that a walnut shell over there on the ground? I didn't think walnut trees grew around here. But there it was, an empty half shell. Picking it up, I peered inside: the ridges rough and prickly to the touch and colored in varied shades of brown. Once it must have tightly gripped an enclosed nut forcing it to conform exactly to those convoluted ridges. Unexpected tears formed in my eyes. Like that walnut, I'd been confined to a life of rigidity, but there'd be no escape for me. My final vows to God were made for life. Just then I heard a rustle in the branches overhead and looked up to see a bird soar straight up to the sky. My tears spilled over.

Mercifully those three years of worsening loneliness ended, and I was given permission to study. I'd always been drawn to psychology and counseling and now I'd get my Masters degree if I could accomplish that feat in one year. I called it my *Gift Year* since every day was filled with beneficent surprises. Because I'd be doing my internship at a state university, I was allowed to wear regular clothes and not my religious habit, so I wrote my three younger sisters and asked facetiously if they'd join the *Adopt-A-Nun Program.* For the first time in nineteen years, I'd be wearing colors other than black, white, grey or navy blue. I loved trying on what they sent me: a brown skirt, pink blouse, green pants, but I was shaken when I saw my reflection in the mirror wearing a red pullover sweater. I wasn't yet ready to wear the color red. After being cooped up for years in a ponytail under my veil, my hair was thrilled; it was now out, free and bouncing in the sunlight.

I remembered the day back when my Postulant year was coming to an end. A sign went up instructing the 9 of us who still remained from our original 17, to report to a certain large room in the building where the professed Sisters lived apart from us who were in training. Since it was a Silence Day, we walked over without being able to share our curiosity but by now were used to refraining from conversation. After all in just a few days, we would go through a ceremony to become *Novices,* trading in our mid-calf black Postulant dresses with short black veils which revealed snippets of our hair and individuality for full-length Novice's black *habits* with an extra large black rosary entwined around a white rope belt and an amazing white veil. We'd already learned how to put together that veiled contraption which would go over our heads like a helmet of hard starched white linen, pins, and heavy white veiling. Only our framed faces and exposed hands would evidence our uniqueness, but that was the point. We would lose ourselves for the sake of Christ. We would be nuns.

When we entered the room that day, we saw nine raised stools and a professed Sister with a scissors standing next to each one. A towel was draped around our shoulders as we looked around in shock and powerlessness. No one spoke. Since there were no mirrors, the only way I could visualize what was happening to me was to see the shearing of the other girls. Big tufts of hair cascaded to the floor. I could see my *Summer Blonde* had faded back to mousy brown. Theresa's thick coarse Navajo hair and Christine's Afro and Carole's fine Filipina hair and Eileen's black Irish curls joined my locks with the other girls' making a strange carpet on the wooden floor. After a while we stopped looking at each other, as if not wanting to see one another naked. Our heads weren't shaved; we were just given buzz cuts so our heads wouldn't swelter under those unyielding veils.

This is what I recalled when I shook loose my pony tail that day, nineteen years later. Over the years the veils had been modified and now even showed a little hair. They were loose enough to let each woman maintain her hair as she decided best, but still they were always worn. Now, my whole head felt light and giddy!

Autumn came and I gloried in the wooded path behind my graduate dorm as leaves wafted their smells and hues for my delight. Every day was a celebration, a liberation. People called me *Mary* not *Sister* and I got to role-play clinical cases with my classmates amidst both tears and laughter.

I learned to swim laps at the campus Fitness Center and joined my classmates once a week at a restaurant with a dance floor. After those 12-hour class days, my friends gleefully relished the chance to fling arms and legs to the pounding beat while I sat self-consciously watching them and sipping my coke. Then one evening undetected, I got up, found a shadowed corner and just let the music course through me. Gradually my sway took on more and more movement until I finally let go with abandon. I never watched from the sidelines again.

Not long afterward, many of us students took part in a several mile CROP Walk to raise money and awareness to combat hunger. That's when I first met John, a missionary priest stationed in South America who was getting his counseling degree before returning. I was taken by his soft curly hair and gentle brown eyes and felt warm inside as he walked quietly beside me. Just when I'd mustered the courage to speak to him however, he excused himself saying he had to get back to campus and then disappeared into the crowd. I felt a curious mixture of delight and disappointment but also had the nagging thought these feelings were not allowed. Some days later John called to ask if I'd join him for some racquetball. When I protested I didn't know how to play, he offered to teach me and so we met at the campus courts where he demonstrated the rudiments of the game. My skills and stamina were way below his but I was loathe to relinquish any time with him and forced myself to play game after game. When I ate dinner that evening with my suitemates, my arms were so sore, I had to use both hands to lift a glass of water. I was inordinately happy.

He and I began to seek each other out between classes and at campus events even as I was tormented by self-accusations: *Are you just being naïve? Are you walking down a dangerous path? Will God be angry with you?* I approached my closest friend in the program, a nun my own age on sabbatical from her missionary work in Africa, and asked if I could speak to her in confidence. She listened to my joy in growing closer to John as well as to my concerns which were growing as well. *Mary, you've never dated anyone in your adult life, so maybe you need to know what you're giving up before you can freely choose a life of celibacy.* She also presented the possibility that John and I could be spiritual friends like Francis and Clare of Assisi, or John of the Cross and Teresa of Avila, priest/nun pairs who expressed their mutual love by encouraging each other to live well their separate religious vocations.

Now I had even more thoughts swirling in my head and looked for the first opportunity to talk them over with John. We met at a nearby lake where I opened my heart to him. John then shared his affection for me and added, *It's a good thing you're committed to staying in religious life because if you ever left, I'd have to seriously consider leaving the priesthood.* I was thrilled to hear of his feelings for me but absolutely confident I'd never leave the convent thus ensuring his priesthood was not in jeopardy. When we arrived back at my dorm in his junker of a car, John turned off the ignition, leaned across the seat and kissed me. I went to my room in a daze of emotions.

July 4th marked the last day of our graduate program. A bunch of us newly minted counselors brought picnic baskets and blankets to the local park and happily plopped down, friends and classmates together for the last time. John and I were acutely aware of each other in the rowdy mix but continued in the collective camaraderie. Slowly the sky darkened as we finished off our meal in trailing conversations, waiting for the fireworks to begin. Suddenly a single lit streak shot across the night sky accompanied by an eerie whistling sound. Then, silence. We held our breaths until it came: an explosion of color splattering the black canvas like a Jackson Pollard painting while a chorus of ooh's and ah's erupted on the ground. As the rainbow sparks continued to rain down on us, I felt the warmth of another's hand encircling mine. I looked up and saw John holding me in his eyes.

Almost immediately I was to fly to Arizona to teach 8th grade at a school staffed by our Sisters on a Navajo reservation there, an assignment communicated to me a few weeks earlier. Before leaving, I made an appointment with my spiritual director, a good man and holy priest who ran a retreat center in my home state of NJ, someone who'd been my trusted advisor for years. I spoke the truth to Bill, not only about my relationship with John, but also about the suffocating grief which was settling upon me. He spoke words I didn't expect: *Mary, this sounds like marital love you're describing.* I panicked and protested, *No! I'm describing a love like Francis and Clare! I've made vows to God and I can't break them. I can survive in the convent!* He looked at me with great kindness, *God doesn't want you just to survive, Mary. God wants you to live.* Then he quoted Scripture: *I put before you a blessing and a curse, life and death. Choose life.*

I left Bill's office deeply shaken. He'd suggested a plan for me and thought I might want to share it with John. Take this coming year as a time of discernment. Stay in contact with each other through letter and cassette tape while asking God in prayer what it means for each of you to *choose life.* I managed to reach John before he left for South America but he seemed distracted, more focused on his weeks ahead in Language School than on this recommended year of discernment. His responses were vague and unsatisfying, and I had to remind myself of Bill's closing words: *This is about you, Mary. It's not about John. He's responsible for his own discernment; you need to discover what choosing life means for you.*

A month after my *Gift Year* ended, I stepped back into religious life, donning my habit, covering my hair with a veil, and answering again to *Sister.* It did not go well. I tried to immerse myself in Navajo culture and attempted to reclaim enthusiasm for teaching. I discovered the desert did indeed have a stark beauty and the native people I met were gracious and welcoming, but my heart was ashen as I slipped into depression with these overwhelming changes. I was facing failure yet again. Since I'd previously been stationed in African-American communities, the Sisters in leadership thought I'd flourish in a more familiar culture and so transferred me to Harlem. There I was asked to teach music in grades 1-8 and I prayed for strength and courage each time I pushed open a classroom door with my guitar in hand. The students were wonderfully responsive, the Sisters extraordinarily kind but my inner darkness only deepened.

John never wrote. I continued to send letters and an occasional tape but there was no reply. I met with a nun psychotherapist and told her of my discernment process: whether to stay in religious life or leave. Was God calling me to recommit as a Sister or put myself in a position where I could pursue marriage? Perhaps that woman was struggling with her own issues of commitment but she absolutely told me I should stay in the convent and not even consider breaking my vows.

I left her office and did not go back. I did, however, find solace in the compassion of the local Director (no longer called Mother Superior) of that Harlem convent who listened tenderly as I shared my spiritual wrestling and offered me encouragement when day after day, no message came from John.

Really I did know what to do to choose life - I was just afraid to do it. It was 1986, I was 38 years old and had been in the convent more than half my life. How could I make it *out in the world* with no money, no regular clothes, no job, no car, no credit record, no resume, no references, no place to live, no furniture, no support network, and no savvy about what it'd be like to be on my own as a single woman in the mid-1980's? Even though I longed to be in a loving relationship, I knew that a sexual revolution had taken place since the days when I was a chaste high school girl exchanging a few kisses with her boyfriend in the back seat of his parents' car while his Dad kept an eye on us in his rear view mirror. What mature man would want to be with a woman who had the naivete of a teenager? And if I left, how would this impact those who knew and loved me: my parents, siblings, former students and their families, the other Sisters? How disillusioning would it be for me, the former *Recruiter*, to be leaving the very congregation she invited young women to join just a few years before?

Yet despite this boulder of fear pressing me down to stay, I remembered the promise I'd made to God on a blustery October day a few weeks earlier. Some former classmates from my counseling program wanted to pick me up and take me to New England for a Fall Foliage weekend. Since they were afraid to drive into Harlem, they asked if I could meet them across the river at Newark Airport. The Sisters I was living with urged me to take a bus and meet my friends as they could see my depression was winning. Robotically, I went and found myself leaning against the outside wall of the terminal, staring thoughtlessly at a bleak sky on a cold overcast day. A question slowly formed in my mind: *Do you want to still choose life?* I wasn't suicidal, but I was weary of the effort it took to get up each day. Several moments passed before the answer slipped into my awareness. There were no alleluias attached but I did manage an anemic *yes.*

So in early December, I picked up the phone and called the Sister President of my congregation to say I wanted to leave. She resisted this and tried to dissuade me but I was firm. Finally she discussed with me the process of leaving. I would need to write to Rome to get released from my vows and this could be a slow process. In the meantime, I'd have to alert the local bishop of my presence wherever I found a place to live. He would be the person I'd officially be *obedient* to until my papers were finalized. She told me I wasn't to date while still bound by the vow of *chastity,* and I would need to keep honoring my vow of *poverty* which I thought would be unavoidable given my circumstances. She said the congregation would give me $1000 as a parting gift and loan me some money interest free. She then asked if I were happy now. I thought about her question and after a pause answered truthfully, *No, not yet, but I'm at peace.*

Five days before Christmas, two Sisters from the Harlem convent drove me out of NYC to the empty retreat house in New Jersey, where my spiritual advisor Bill had a room available for me until after the holidays. It was understood I'd leave there by January 2ⁿᵈ when the retreat center would be full again. During the interim I needed to get a job, a car, an apartment, furniture and some non-nun clothes. I was staggered by the enormity of these tasks. Each day I set out resolutely on foot to find an apartment, but no one would rent to me without proof of a job. I tried to get a job, but no one would hire me without a permanent address. Finally through a contact of Bill's, I landed a minimum wage job working in a greenhouse which would begin January 3rd.

Armed with this information and borrowing his car on the last weekday I could stay at the retreat house, I drove to as many apartment complexes as I could find. With daylight waning, I made my way into the office of a rather run-down facility. The woman at the desk was about seven months pregnant and smoking a cigarette. She recited by rote the rental details and seemed quite bored until I interrupted her spiel with a question. She had just told me the security deposit would be the same as the first month's rent when I, puzzled, asked, *Do I have to pay for the security guard too?* That brought her to an upright position and she took the cigarette out of her mouth saying, *Where are you from anyway?* My mask of competence crumpled and through my tears I explained my desperation. Without commenting on my woeful tale, she pushed a key toward me and said I could move in that Sunday. No one would be in the office so just let myself into the efficiency. She never offered to show me the apartment and I didn't know to ask. I was overjoyed and relieved to have a place to go and prayed her baby would be born healthy.

My parents had been stunned when I told them over the phone I'd be leaving the convent. I think it brought them shame as my being a nun was a source of pride and blessing for them within our family and among their friends. We agreed it would not be good for me to move back in and live with them, as I wanted to discover who I was as my own person. Dad picked me up at the retreat house on December 25th and I celebrated Christmas once more in my parents' home with my siblings and our extended family. My sisters had taken the lead and were gathering clothes, sheets, towels and furniture from their own homes to help me get started in mine. When I called and shared my pressing deadline, they were ready.

Early that Sunday morning, my siblings and parents formed a caravan of loaded-down vehicles and picked me up at the retreat center where we then proceeded to the apartment complex. Shaking with anticipation, I turned the key to my efficiency and swung open the door. It was horrible. The room was unkempt, filthy and cheap, with one bare light bulb dangling from a cord in the ceiling, chicken bones in the kitchenette sink and unidentified things floating in the toilet. My sisters got out scrub brushes and soapy water, the men spackled the walls and moved in the furniture and my mother put her arm around me in the middle of the room and let me cry. When they left, I was alone for the first time in my own little home which now sparkled with their love.

I lay in bed that night and talked to God: *My Beloved, thank you, thank you, thank you. We made it. Stay with me tomorrow when I start my new job. I'm scared but I know you didn't bring me this far to leave me.*

I had three priorities: 1) make enough money for food and rent; 2) start paying back the money I borrowed from the Sisters and my parents; 3) look for someone to share my life and love with.

The first two were tough but I was gradually able to move from minimum wage jobs to one that was salaried which helped me chip away at my debts. But the third goal would. I had to let go of the fantasy that John and I would be together, and then, since God hadn't provided a Prince Charming waiting for me at the convent gate, I had to seek actively for a relationship. I joined dating clubs and discussion groups, filled out questionnaires, went to singles events and took dance lessons. One year went by. Two. Three.

And still I was single. *God, this isn't what I expected! Going through all this to leave the convent only to live alone for the rest of my life!*

Finally at the age of forty-one, I surrendered. *Okay, God, you win. Maybe this is what you had in mind for me all along, to be single. Help me be at peace with this. From now on, instead of constantly searching, I'll simply savor life.* That was on a Monday. The following Saturday I went to a *Sock Hop for Singles* I'd read about in the local paper. Since I loved to dance, this would be a great way for me to savor without searching. So I went to the church hall, took my little Styrofoam cup of tea to each table and introduced myself, *Hi, I'm Mary. I just moved into the area and I love to dance. It's really nice to meet you all.* What a great time I had! I danced every dance, met lots of fun people and told God this wasn't half-bad.

Then the DJ directed a dance formation with rotating partners and when it ended announced, *Whoever you're with right now is going to be your partner for the dance contest.* I looked questioningly at the stranger across from me who nodded *yes* while extending his hand, *Hi, I'm Carl.* Tall, slender and tan with blonde hair and blue eyes, he wasn't someone I'd seen earlier when making my table rounds. Later I learned he'd just stopped by the church hall to pick up some tickets when someone pulled him onto the dance floor. Before the night was over, we'd won first prize in the dance contest and exchanged phone numbers. It had started to rain by the time we walked out, the last ones to leave the building, and he shielded me with his umbrella on the way to the parking lot. When I drove off with him watching me leave safely, I could hardly wait to talk to him again. Over the days and weeks that followed, we grew to like each other even more and I began to wonder if he was just too good to be true.

Then one day I got a phone call from his mother whom I'd yet to meet. She asked, *You know how Carl seems to be so kind?* I answered *yes* and waited for the other shoe to drop, but instead she said, *Well that's the way he really is.*

I shared with Carl that I had been a nun, and he wondered if that would prevent our dating. We both had Irish roots, but his were Protestant and mine Catholic – and that mattered a great deal at one time. Carl's Dad had once dated a Catholic girl named Agnes Kelly, but the relationship was called off due to their religious differences. Even though his family had stopped going to church long before Carl was born and he'd never been baptized, there was still a wariness toward Catholics just as in my family, there was resistance to marrying outside the faith.

But any concerns I had personally were assuaged early in our relationship when Carl asked over dinner one evening, *Mary, I know prayer is really important to you and I've heard you mention meditation. I want to know more. What is prayer like for you?* Then he settled back to listen to what was deepest in my heart. I in turn asked about his experience of The Holy as someone who'd never had any exposure to church or religion. We both valued the other's spirituality and felt enriched in the sharing. I even chuckled at Carl's response when a non-Catholic friend of his was trying to fill in the blanks about my mysterious background, *Oh God had her salted away in the convent for me.*

There was a stunning sunset one January evening as we walked across a pedestrian bridge spanning the Delaware River between our two states of New Jersey and Pennsylvania. White clouds parted overhead to reveal a palette of aqua, pink and orange which was reflected in the icy waters below. Carl leaned in close to me and said, *Mary, I wanted to pick a place that shows how you and I have come together from two different places. Will you marry me?* My legs were shaky but my heart was strong, *Oh yes!* They all came to our wedding: his family and mine, his friends and mine, and we had a choir of 10 nuns singing to our happiness in glorious harmony.

We've been together 26 years now, Carl and I, and our love has deepened through the joys and challenges of marriage. We didn't have children of our own but eventually volunteered once a month at a facility for severely impaired children, most of whom were on ventilators. With our guitars slung over our shoulders, we'd stop at each kid's bed and serenade the little one in front of us. We also continue to delight in the relationships we have with our many nieces and nephews. Whether dancing with babies at family gatherings, hiding Easter eggs in my parents' backyard for the annual kids' scramble, being a pen pal with several of the middle-schoolers, or seeking conversation and connection with the young adults, Carl and I have learned that *aunt* and *uncle* are sacred words.

But what about loneliness, my frequent companion and nemesis for so many years? Has Carl's presence banished this unwelcome guest? Curiously, no. I've discovered that dealing with loneliness is my responsibility. For too long I believed that doing wonderful things for others or being in a great relationship with someone would remove the terrible ache of separateness. But really the ache had more to do with the division inside of me. For most of my life, I'd been trying to live the identity of a movie character I'd seen as a kid: *Mary Poppins, practically perfect in every way!* When I finally recognized and accepted the real Mary: flawed, funny, sexual, over-functioning, caring, impulsive, needy, loving, I was able to feel safe within myself. Now I wasn't desperate for someone else to love me and make me whole. With God's grace, I could do that myself. What freedom when I finally understood the two most forgotten words of Jesus: *Love your neighbor <u>as</u> <u>yourself</u>.*

During those years of living on his own, Carl came to a similar realization on his life's journey: better to find contentment within myself than to search frantically for someone or something to *make me happy.* So finding each other brought richness to both of us without either of us having to rescue or be rescued by the other.

Every day we thank God for the unexpected gift of this relationship and we treat it with care. In both word and gesture, we often express our love, gratitude and goodwill to each other, and when the inevitable hurts and misunderstandings arise between us, we hope each of us can *hold onto* ourselves until our feeling of connection is restored. In our marriage we see ourselves, not as two halves making a whole, but as two wholes making a pretty good duo walking through life side by side.

Amen. Alleluia.

THE PRETTY GREEN STICK
BY MEGAN EMILY

During first semester freshman year, I sat behind David in Honors Old Testament at our small Wesleyan university. He had a broken leg and came to class in his bathrobe and wheelchair, but I was too busy staring at his blonde hair, blue eyes, and broad shoulders to notice. When David spoke up in class, he raised his hand with a blue pen between his fingers, leaned toward the professor, and took careful notes in thin, slanted handwriting.

We started dating the following April. David was what I was looking for: a tall, blonde country boy who loved God. I thought it was adorable that he'd wanted to be a preacher since he was four years old.

Before David, I'd never had a Christian boyfriend. My most serious relationship was when I was in high school. Nick was a friend of my sister; he was well out of high school and worked with racehorses, studying to be a jockey. I went out with him for the first time on my seventeenth birthday. His humor was too crass and his hands roamed too much during the movie, but I neverthe-less said yes when he asked me out again. I wanted to make sure I wasn't just writing him off because of his size – at four feet, nine inches tall, he was more than a head shorter than me.

During our second date, Nick's mom died. I was with him when he got the phone call, with him all through the night. I stayed with him for the months of his grieving process, hoping to help him even when I wasn't sure his drinking and drug use had anything to do with grief. Our relationship was so intense that I never questioned sleeping with Nick.

I'd grown up in church. Pastors, youth leaders – all men – told me pre-marital sex was a sin, but I wondered what happened if I was in love, if I was going to marry the man. I thought Nick and I could make an exception. I was already wearing a ring on my left hand, a promise ring to stand in until he proposed for real, so in my mind, we had no reason to wait.

Our relationship was punctuated with his lies, our lovemaking, and his ever-present bottle of pain pills, bought illegally from a classmate. I was in love with him because he needed me, because he said I made him a better person. But what he meant was, he *wanted* me to make him a better person, to make him happy, be-cause he wasn't able to be happy on his own. I stumbled under the weight of his expectations, especially when he started lashing out at me. In public, he called me names or made fun of my appear-ance. In bed, he told me he loved me.

By the time he started publicly criticizing me, he'd stopped say-ing, "I love you, I don't know what I'd do without you." Instead, he told me, "If we ever broke up, I'd kill myself." I spent three months – the latter half of our relationship – working up the courage to leave. I hated him for manipulating me with suicide threats, for putting his life on my shoulders when I was barely old enough to be responsible for myself. It took two years for me to forgive Nick, and another year before I could remember how, sometimes, he had made me laugh or held my hand in the car or told me I was pretty.

Dating David was like stepping outside after a rainstorm, inhaling the fresh scent of the trees as water droplets glistened on flower petals. Unlike Nick, who rarely spoke of God, David worked at his faith. I admired that.

Like David, I grew up in the church. I'd always believed in God and, except for those few months in high school, I'd tried to live by the Bible. I wanted to be a good Christian girlfriend, to respect David and build him up. But I had no idea how to do that. Especially since supporting Nick had been complicated, often putting me in compromising situations.

After we broke up, I regretted sleeping with Nick – not because I believed what I'd done was so wrong, but because my religion told me that I was worthless without my virginity. Thinking what I'd done was irreparable, I slept with two other men. I no longer valued myself enough to say no. Losing my self-worth was what I regretted most. It took two years – right up until I met David – to forgive myself.

I wanted to have an honest relationship with David, so I told him about my past. He promised it wasn't an issue; he was a recovering porn addict. We decided to set physical boundaries so we could protect ourselves: I wanted to wait for marriage before I had sex again, and David didn't want to risk the progress he'd made in his recovery or, worse in his eyes, lose his virginity. However, because sex had been an integral part of my relationship with Nick, I had no idea what boundaries to set with David. I told him, "You think about what boundaries you want, and whatever you decide, I'll follow." I left making the rules to him, because I'd been told good Christian girls let their man be the head of the relationship.

As a result, our boundaries seemed arbitrary. David picked December 10 for our first kiss – not because the date was meaningful to us, but because two of his friends planned to have their first kiss on December 10. I had no regrets when we broke the rules early, in May. Kissing was now allowed.

In theory, according to David's boundaries, our physical relationship ended at kissing. In practice, we weren't so sure of ourselves. We emphasized physical purity because that was what we were supposed to do, but what we'd learned in church about respecting each other could basically be summed up with, "Just say no." Soon, our relationship's main goal was "to not have sex with each other." We were so hyper-aware of the sexual tension between us, it was hard not to cross the lines we set for ourselves. Every three weeks, like clockwork, David sat me down to "have a talk" about our physical boundaries and reset them because we'd moved them around again.

Sometimes he complained that I kissed him too much. But if I smudged our boundaries, David erased them. Once, a couple of months after we started dating, I was the one who remembered to stop when he rolled on top of me. I pulled away. We were outdoors in the middle of the night, lying on a blanket to stargaze. "Let's just look at the sky," I said. After another minute, he was back on top of me. I put a hand on his chest and pushed him away. This time, I said, "No." I told him no that time, and when he groped me, and when he pulled my shirt up, until I got sick of him ignoring me. So I shut myself off, staring blankly at the stars while he did what he wanted.

He stopped before we had sex, collapsing onto my chest in tears. "This is wrong," he sobbed. "I can't do this." He was grieving for experiencing several sexual firsts outside of marriage.

I put my arms around him. "It's okay," I murmured. It would be over a year before I realized I had been violated, before I cried.

It wasn't a surprise that our first fight had to do with sex. As we walked around campus, David confessed to looking at porn the night before. I stayed quiet a minute, thinking of ways to help. Finally, I asked, "Do you have any guys you can talk to? I love you, but I'm a 20-year-old girl. I can't mentor you through this." I even named a handful of older male professors and pastors I knew David respected. "Why don't you text one of them?" I asked.

"Because, I'm ashamed," he said. He was afraid if anyone knew he struggled with porn addiction, it would ruin his reputation as a man of God. Somehow, he'd come to believe that in order to be a pastor – or even a ministerial student – he could only have "appropriate" struggles, like mentoring his little brother or learning to read the New Testament in its original Greek. Porn addiction wasn't a positive struggle, so he had to hide it.

"It's the same reason I don't tell anyone about your past," he added. I froze. David knew I'd had sex, but I hadn't ever told him how I felt about it. I hadn't told him how many times I'd encouraged other Christian girls who were ashamed of losing their virginity, how I told them God still loved them, or how happy I was to see those girls start to heal because I shared what I'd been through. I'd thought David didn't talk about my past out of respect for me – not to protect himself. Unable to look at him, I watched a bug crawling on the sidewalk. If my boyfriend was ashamed of something I'd done before our relationship – something God had already forgiven me for – then it wasn't just my behavior he had a problem with. He was embarrassed by me, by who I was.

But I thought it would be selfish to tell him how hurtful his words were, when he was feeling so guilty for last night's mistake. Instead, I made him take out his phone and text a pastor to set up a meeting. Once he promised to contact at least one professor when he returned to his room, I cuddled up to him on the bench where we sat. He held my hand on the way back to my dorm.

Lying in bed later that night, I was seething. I glared at the ceiling until two in the morning, when I finally texted David what was on my mind. I ended with, "You made me feel shittier tonight than Nick ever did." He knew Nick had lied to me about money, gotten black-out drunk, and called me fat every time we ate together.

Comparing him to Nick was the only way I could think of to make him understand how much he'd hurt me.

Although I refused to speak to David for two days, I accepted his apology when we did meet up. "I was afraid you were going to break up with me," he said.

"I thought about it." I hadn't done it, because I wanted to marry him. Letting go of his words would show him how committed I was to our relationship. Besides, we had been together for almost six months; I reasoned that it was about time for the honeymoon phase to end.

We went on as if nothing had happened. I sat in the ministry building with David between his classes, editing the grammar in his papers. He bought me lunch and brought it to me at work when I didn't have time to eat. But underneath, I could feel the strain. It tugged at us like mud drying into hard clay, cracking open under the sun's glare.

For fall break, I invited David home with me. I thought three days on my parents' farm would be relaxing. Instead, the trip toppled the uneasy peace between us, like pulling the wrong peg out of a Jenga tower.

It started with the tree. I'd gone shopping with my mom and older sister. As Mom's truck bounced back up our rutted driveway, we waved out the window to the guys – my dad, my brother-in-law, and a man we had hired to help cut up an old, rotten maple tree. The three of them had been working on it all day. When we walked into the house with our shopping bags, David – who had ostensibly stayed home to do homework – was sitting on the couch watching *Spongebob*.

I didn't mind him taking a break. He spent far more time studying than I ever did. But when I'd been visiting his family last month, the industrial air compressor his stepdad used for working on semi-trucks had blown out. I knew nothing about air compressors or diesel mechanics, and Bruce was a burly, bearded man who scared me with his angry silence. I ventured into the garage any-way and offered to drive into the nearest city, forty minutes away, to pick up any replacement parts from the machine shop. My par-ents had raised me to help people, especially when those people were my significant other's family.

I put my shopping bags in my room, changed into my work boots, and grabbed a pair of leather gloves. So did Mom and Elizabeth. When I walked back into the living room, David looked up. "Where are you going?"

"Out to help with the tree."

"Oh, okay."

"It might be nice if you'd come out and help, too," I hinted.

He looked at me, his face blank. "It's too cold out," he said.

I stared at him. It was the middle of October, the thermometer perched at fifty-five degrees. I put a hand on my hip. "No, it's not," I said. "My family is letting you sleep in their house and eat their food. So you're going to get up, and you're going to put your coat on, and you're going to come out and help us."

David turned off the TV and came outside. For several hours, we dragged sawed-off pieces of brush over to the burn pile beside the driveway. Dad and the hired man sawed the bigger branches and trunk into firewood, which we stacked in the truck bed to take to a neighbor who had a wood-burning stove. All seven of us joked and cut up while we worked, enjoying the fall weather. I noticed David's jacket where he'd left it, hanging on a nearby fence post.

The tree under control, I went to the barn with my mom and sister to take care of our horses. David headed back up the hill to the house. "I'm not an animal person," he said.

I shoveled manure out of my horse's stall. When I was thirteen, my parents had bought a half-starved, head-shy project horse be-cause he was all we could afford. I spent all of middle school and half of high school turning him into a show jumper – not easy when I had just started riding. Six years later, Chance was the best riding horse my family had.

It was an adrenaline rush to fly for a split second, to know Chance trusted me to guide him. I couldn't think of a way to tell David what it was like to bond with Chance, fifteen years after my little sister died in a freak accident with a horse. Learning to ride again was like an ice-water glass of redemption.

As I saddled Chance, I glared at the house. I wished David would just let me give him a riding lesson. Or that when he came home with me, he would stop putting his arms around me every time we walked by the pasture and saying, "She's mine now, Chance." I hated that he didn't understand how important my horse was to me – or worse, that he didn't seem to care.

After riding, I fed Chance a treat and gave him a good chest-scratching before letting him out into the pasture with the other horses. I was mad at David for not coming to the barn, but when I got to the house, he was sitting at the snack bar, textbooks open. "Go look on your bed," he said.

A teddy bear sat on my pillow holding my favorite singer's latest album, a bag of Skittles, and a card. Inside the card was a hand-written note, saying how much he loved me and how lucky he was to have me for a girlfriend. I put the gifts back on the bed and walked out to the kitchen, putting my arms around his neck and kissing his cheek. "I love you," I said.

Later, after we had gone to our separate rooms for the night, I texted David to ask him to come cuddle with me. He waited until the house was quiet, then snuck into my bed. At first, when I started to take off his t-shirt, he stopped me. I apologized and snuggled up to him, my head on his chest. The second time we started kissing, it took longer to stop. A small pile of clothes lay rumpled on the floor.

I expected him to be upset that we'd come so close to having sex, but the next night, he snuck into my room again. I wished he hadn't – for once, I was the one who thought we'd gone too far the night before. His sneaking into my room two nights in a row made me feel like he now expected anything-but-sex. I was tired of expectations. In spite of that, I still played hooky with him on Sunday morning, crawling into bed with him even though a voice in my head told me not to.

I wanted to be more physical, but right now, it felt like I was trying to use physical intimacy to patch up fissures in our relationship. Like how, lately, I was angry at David – for things like the tree, or taunting Chance, or not taking me out when all I wanted to do was go dancing.

We were in the honors study house the Saturday after break, sitting on a stiff-backed couch. I stared at the industrial blue carpet. He told me neither of us had been doing well with God lately – which was true – but that he had repented for what happened over break. Now it was my turn. "You need to fix your relationship with God," he said. "It's hurting our dating relationship."

I wanted to tell him that wasn't how it worked, that my relationship with God wasn't a tool to make me a better girlfriend. I wanted to say that if he saw me struggling, he should have prayed for me or asked what was wrong. Last summer, when we went swimming in a lake, I got trapped underwater. When I surfaced, retching and gasping, David wrapped an arm around my waist, treading water for both of us. I wanted to ask why he wasn't doing that now. Instead, I said nothing. I'd watched him flail the last few weeks – I hadn't offered to pray for him, either.

So I sat still, feeling the coarse hairs of his arm press against my skin as he stood up. When he said my value on purity wasn't high enough, I stayed silent. He stopped pacing to stand in front of me, looking down at me. "I know that's not your fault," he said. "You were never taught any better."

I clenched my jaw. It was true that no one in my family had been a virgin on their wedding day, but my parents had a rock-solid marriage, somehow grown even stronger in the wake of my little sister's death. My older sister was married to the only man she'd ever dated – and I'd just found out yesterday that she was pregnant with their first baby. To me, purity was more than sex. It was being committed to one person, and only that one.

Anger constricted my chest, clutching my ribs tight against my lungs. So I let it out. "You have no right to bring up my family right now," I snapped. "What they did is between them and God, just like what I did was between me and God. And for your information, they weren't happy about what I did. They were mad at me for weeks because they want me to do better and not repeat their mistakes. You leave my family out of this, do you understand me?"

He barely nodded, already pacing in front of me again. Suddenly I was five years old, and he was the adult, the male authority whose job it was to admonish me.

According to David, he was the one doing the most to make the relationship work. I wanted to point out that he was also the one who had snuck into my room the second time, the one who had asked me to do more to pleasure him Sunday morning because what I was doing "wasn't working anymore." Instead, I stared at my jeans and at the ugly pattern on that stupid, uncomfortable couch.

When he paused to take a breath, I looked into his eyes.

"I'm never going to be good enough for you, am I?" I wasn't asking.

He said nothing.

I walked out. Later, I apologized. We kept trying to make our relationship work, but we both knew it was over. I cringed when he touched me, or snapped at him for asking about my day. I used to comfort him when his mom guilt-tripped him for not visiting home enough. Now I told him she was controlling and manipulative. I wore his class ring in front of her to make her mad, to provoke his family because he had attacked mine.

David and I decided not to see each other over Thanksgiving break. We didn't say it, but we were both exhausted from trying to hold our relationship together. When he called me Thursday night, I knew what he wanted.

"I think we should break up," he said.

I let out the breath I'd been holding for a month. "Me too."

Once again, I had to forgive a man I used to love. The difference is that I wanted to hurt David – not because he wasn't the Christian man I hoped for, but because he blamed me for not being the Christian woman he thought I should be.

I'm realizing now that I probably won't ever be that woman. The church encouraged me to be good – to respect David, to support him, to let him lead me. But no one ever told me how to do any of those things. As a result, I believed that to be the Ideal Woman, I had to tone down who I was. I ignored my own feelings to build David up. I sacrificed my identity trying to be a good Christian girlfriend – when I only had a shaky idea of how to have a healthy relationship – and I ended up hurting both of us.

Forgiving David is harder than forgiving Nick. In Nick's case, I was dating an alcoholic who had lost both parents by the time he was twenty-one; that relationship was bound to have problems. I saw some of that pain coming. But I thought a ministry student would be more sensitive, more compassionate; maybe, more healing. I wasn't prepared for David to control the clothes I wore or music I listened to, claiming he wanted to make sure I was being modest, or to criticize my faith. I had admired him and was surprised that he did not value my admiration.

Sometimes, Christians talk about loss of virginity like it's the worst thing that could happen to a woman. "It's like you've lost all the petals from your flower," as one of my friends described it.

When my older sister Elizabeth was a toddler, she plucked a flower. She played with it, shaking it until all the petals fell off. Mom looked over and saw Elizabeth's face puckered up. Before she could launch a scream-and-cry fit, Mom smiled at her and said, "Look at that pretty green stick you made!" Elizabeth looked at the naked stem in her hand, then grinned and went right back to playing with it. She was delighted with it for what it was – even if it was a little different.

For the second time I'm learning to love myself again, to forgive myself. Most of all, I'm learning to appreciate who I am – a believer in Jesus who is beautiful whether she has a dozen petals or none at all.

⭆ ⭅

HAUNTED HONEYMOON
BY LAURA ENGLE

My husband and I met in at the Capital View Health Care Center in Salem, Oregon. I directed activities and he worked as a Willamette University music therapy intern. My standard joke is that we were the only two datable people in the place, so we had no choice but to get together. The truth, however, is more subtle.

I remember sizing him up the day we met. His teachers had warned me, "If he gives you any trouble of any kind, call us." When I interviewed him, he seemed nice enough. I noted with amusement that he had a pillow crease on is face, evidence that he had been asleep maybe only minutes before he arrived. His long hair and artistic clothes were not your typical frat boy attire: a good sign, it seemed to me. He carried a guitar. I was only recently from southern California and, in retrospect, I think he reminded me of the place. In fact, had we been in California conducting that first interview I probably would have written him off immediately.

Down there guys like him either wouldn't go for me, were trouble, or maybe both. But we were in Salem and I was a long way from home. Something about him spoke to my homesickness.

We started dating and got married right away, "to please his conservative grandparents," he said, and I was a classic "good girl" anyway. We eloped, however, so things were a little dicey in the realm of pleasing family, especially grandparents. We couldn't afford to honeymoon, so instead we decided to visit my grandparents in California as soon as we could. I had a lot riding on the visit; my grandmother was the only person besides my dad whose opinion of Todd mattered to me. Without having ever met Todd, she allowed us to come home and stay with her and Grandpa and, just like every other older woman who has ever met my husband, she took an immediate liking to him. "Still waters run deep" she said.

He loved her, too, for the challenging, intelligent, anxious person she was. She expressed her opinions freely and expected others to do the same, but she never wanted to be thrown off balance ever and we all knew the thing to do was agree with her. Todd, however, remained gently curious about her opinions, not necessarily persuaded, and was able to respectfully voice his own opinions. They became friends and garden buddies. After we returned to Oregon she sent him t-shirts in the mail from the thrift store where she volunteered, and plant starts, their roots wrapped in damp paper towels covered by plastic sandwich bags. For years we had a leafy green Prayer Plant of hers that traveled with us as we moved from house to house. It grew nicely and every so often, depending on the light, it bloomed.

Eventually my grandfather died and my grandmother moved to Oregon to be nearer to all of us. She became ill with emphysema and was giving up. She argued with the doctor's orders about how to take care of her lungs. One day I caught her letting the medicine from her nebulizer, her "breathing machine" as she referred to it, escape into the air around her rather than inhaling it into her lungs. When it came time to discuss health care and what she wanted, it was Todd who consoled her and to whom she listened. She chose to enter the nursing home where he worked as a therapist.

Before she died Grandma gave Todd advice on how to develop the music therapy business we had started. We had been well received in the community and though we had many contracts, we still didn't have enough income to pay the bills. She encouraged us to sell the business to our "best customer" – Robison Jewish Home. This advice turned out to be pivotal for Todd who grew into a leader in our industry during his years at Robison.

After we lost Grandma we only visited California two more times. The family had mostly broken up or moved away. My grandparents had been a fulcrum for all of us, and without them there wasn't much reason.

Many years later, twenty-three, to be exact, and just two months after my fiftieth birthday Todd suggested that we go to California for our vacation in early November, thinking it a good idea to "put the girl back in California." And, he suggested, we could finally afford a honeymoon of sorts. I was no longer a girl and I was feeling it, a kind of solemnity affected me, typical of those moments when one is suddenly aware of how much of life has passed and how little time is actually left. "I know!" I said, we can make it a Día de los Muertos tour!

Visiting the Southwest on the cusp of November to take part in a Día de los Muertos celebration had been on my bucket list for a while. In recent years we'd observed the Mexican holiday by going out to a nearby German restaurant and inviting Grandma, now long gone, to a dinner of schnitzel, sausage, and red cabbage. It was Todd's idea. He heard a story about traditional celebrations on NPR and thought it would be fun to summon Grandma. The first time we put food on a plate for her and poured her a little glass of beer, I cried.

We began, then, the first day of our haunted honeymoon, as we had begun to refer to it, in reverence for the passage of time and with thoughts of the many people we have known and loved who have already gone. Many from those long ago California days had passed: teachers, friends, and especially my grandparents. We planned to remember them all and rekindle their spirits if we were able, in the same way those papier mache´ dioramas on the Day of the Dead celebrate shared moments in life. But when we landed, LAX was a crime scene. Someone in a nearby terminal had killed a 35-year-old airport security guard; he had kids at home. It seemed somehow fitting that this first day of the Día de los Muertos celebration is traditionally set aside for los Angelitos, lost children and little innocent ones.

Due to the airport being on lock down, we walked two miles from the airport to our rental car agency. It was warm so I ducked into a fast food restaurant to change from my sweater and boots into a t-shirt and flip flops. This would have been acceptable California attire except that in the busy restaurant surrounded by other refugees from the airport, the only t-shirt I could easily find in my bag was an extra-large, very old shirt that I wear for sleep. It has huge picture of Albert Einstein on the front and the formula for the theory of relativity. The discomfort I felt in my clothes, just then, reminded me of the discomfort I'd felt as a kid wearing hand-me-downs in ritzy Los Angeles. Somehow, reliving that feeling in my Einstein shirt added to the sense of familiarity as I connected with the thin thread of self that weaves in and out of everything, still me but younger for the moment.

Our plans for the day included visiting a raw food restaurant in Santa Monica started by a chef we admired, whose cookbook we have worn to scraps. The delay at LAX slowed us down; did not arrive until 2:30 in the afternoon, shaky and a little frazzled.

The restaurant refreshed us and helped us to forget the day's strange and tragic beginning. When we stepped in, a smell of incense greeted our noses, making us feel we were in a temple as much as a food establishment. A glowing woman with a slender build welcomed us to sit anywhere. She had a vaguely European accent, eyes the color of sea glass, and a small dimple in one cheek; I felt my frayed nerves began to mend and a deep feeling of home washed over me, lighting me up inside with joy and expectancy. We finished our lunch and crossed the street to stroll through a community garden where giant jade plants, bougainvillea, roses, nasturtiums, and a variety of herbs bloomed abundantly, California's version of the winter garden. Some plots still had tomatoes. We could see the blue ocean just beyond the tiled rooftops in the distance. Todd turned to me and in a reverent whisper said, "Why would anyone ever leave this place?" A sense of loss keener than the day my family moved rose in my heart and throat even as one of my grandpa's old jokes came to mind: "My sediments exactly."

We drove up the coast to Ventura; I became calm and quiet during the drive, just taking in the sights and remembering. Teachers and friends I hadn't thought of in years came back to me. Every once in a while I thought I saw someone I knew out of the corner of my eye: my cousin's yellow pigtails trailing behind her in an alley way, my neighbor Peter on his skateboard. I lost all sense of time and felt ready for any of them to return. "Who says you can't go home again?" I wondered aloud.

From Ventura we headed east to Ojai. Ojai is recommended as the place to go if you are looking for "the California depicted on the orange crate." That was exactly the California we hoped to find. I wanted to get the feeling back that I'd had as a kid, only this time with Todd there with me. We a rented small cottage at the Emerald Iguana Inn

The haunted feeling that had set in on me as we headed up the California coast intensified in Ojai. I chalked it up to sights, smells, and air temperatures that were as newly familiar. When we got to our lodging, I opened the window to hear the crickets and lit a fire in the fireplace to get the dampness out of the air just as my grandmother had always done. Without agreeing to it or even thinking about it, we gave up our usual diet of TV and electronics and settled quietly into a routine of cooking dinner at home and sitting by the fire to read in the evenings.

By day we were content to explore, mostly on foot. We tended to drift toward Bart's Books, just a couple of blocks away, an open air bookshop carved out of an old ranchero house. Every day, we found new passageways and hidden rooms to explore. Since the tourist season seemed to be over, we had the place mostly to ourselves. The wall of discarded first-edition children's books from the local library offered some especially inviting reads. I had a very hard time leaving a 1959 first edition of Chanticleer the Rooster for someone else to discover.

We investigated the local farmer's market and coop, an olive ranch, and orange groves, and at night I dreamt of orange groves and hikes in Los Padres National Forest. We met people who by week's end began to feel like old friends. Todd fell into instant rapport with the farmers. One woman, recently widowed, asked him to help her figure out the trees she had growing in the front yard of her new house. Had we stayed any longer, I'm sure she would have offered him work at the olive ranch.

We planned a hike in the Matilija wilderness, a favorite of the locals. Our concierge muttered something about it being a spiritual place. We have such places in the Northwest, many in fact, and the qualifications for "spiritual" elude description. For Todd and me that place is Opal Creek in the Santiam wilderness. We go there to get back to ourselves, in a way, to calibrate. When there, it feels possible to live on a lot less food, with a lot less shelter – preferably, naked. Once I get into that frame of mind I am aware that I am a late comer, an interloper. That realization always causes me to want to invite the brightest light I can imagine: the green in the forest, the organizer who has put every pine needle, nut, bird, and piece of gravel in exactly the right place, to crack me into pieces and do whatever retrofitting is necessary.

Those native to a place have ways of knowing that come from having been a child there, peeking under rocks, and running barefoot over the ground. It is the knowledge that comes from direct experience of the earth itself, testing, exploring, and learning a terrain in the same way we become familiar with the bodies of people we love. The Chumash who lived in the Ojai valley for thousands of years and named it "nest" had revered the Matilija canyon and its healing hot springs. We trusted their understanding of the place and treaded lightly as we entered into their valley.

Now here I was on my native soil, still of a mind to welcome the dead, walking into wilderness that surely contained the remains of the original people who lived on that land not even two hundred years ago. I had no relationship with them, so setting a picnic to welcome them would have been an insult. I did, however, silently ask their permission to enter their world, untouched as it seemed to be, and sort of half expected boulders to roll down the hillsides in answer, "No".

The canyon, however, was empty and took no notice of our arrival. No thing, real or imagined, greeted us. It was as if we stepped back two hundred years into a world unaware of ours and untouched by it. I immediately got the same sense of anonymity that I feel whenever I see a large expanse of ocean or look up at a sky full of stars: no longer me but here.

On the last day of our Día de los Muertos honeymoon, I was determined to be a tourist. I wanted to seek out movie stars and TV locales: especially the bluff where the Dude and Walter said goodbye to Donny in The Big Lebowski and the banana stand where Mr. Bluth from Arrested Development had hidden all of his money. "This is your day," Todd said. "We'll do what you want." "Okay, then," I said, "first stop, Venice Beach! Want to frolic on the beach where Madeline Kahn and Robert Klein got it on in Mixed Nuts?"

We made it to Venice Beach, but instead of frolicking, Todd said "I thought you wanted to go to your home," he said. "Don't you want to go home?"

It's true; I was procrastinating the way that I do when something big is about to happen, or when my heart might get broken, or I am afraid I will fail. I did plan to drive through San Clemente, but I felt reluctant. None of my people live there anymore. No one. I concentrated and tried to get back into the spirit of our quest: welcoming the dead and celebrating our connection.

My cousin told me once, shortly after she was diagnosed with AIDS, that she'd had a dream in which she was visited by Grandma and Grandpa together. They came to her and reassured her that everything was going to be okay. The fact that they appeared together had been important to her, and to me too when she told me about it.

My cousin's ordeal with AIDS was definitely enough to summon the dead and my grandmother's love for all of us was such that if she could come back from beyond to help us, she would. My grandfather was quieter, more reticent and less obtrusive, and in life discounted what he said when he did speak. His mission had been less clear, but his care for us had been consistent. Perhaps their message of reassurance was one reason my cousin has outlived all prognosis for someone with AIDS.

Over the years, in my work with older people, I have been privileged to see and hear things that people believe or know when they are close to death; they tend to talk about it a lot. I have heard many stories in which a loved one appears to someone and offers reassurance. Who knows what is "actually" happening? I've come to accept them as a normal part of human life, but I have never had a dream like that myself, though I have wished for them.

Todd's nudge helped me decide to make a stop in San Pedro, where I knew my grandparents and my mom and uncle had lived when they first arrived in southern California. I had never been to "Pedro" as my grandmother called it, but I had seen some black and white photos from that time in which she appeared particularly vivid and happy. Without any better reason or plan than that, we headed into San Pedro, and that is how we accidentally ended up on the bluff where Walter and the Dude scattered Donny's ashes in The Big Lebowski. It seemed a fitting place to try and connect with Grandpa and Grandma. Grandma had scattered Grandpa's ashes in the Pacific. I stared at the water: so big, so blue, and strangely quiet for all the life and turbulence it contains. I thought of my grandparents but didn't sense them. I wondered about their life there in San Pedro and if they had been happy.

We finally rolled into San Clement as the afternoon light grew pale and the sun was setting. I only wanted to go to North Beach, where we'd spent many days lounging every summer and a part of me has never left. Todd and I parked the car and walked down the path to the beach – paved now, no longer dirt. Lots of things had changed. The sand was gone and thousands of smooth black rocks replaced it. Also, the beach was shorter, much of it actually missing. Standing where we might have once put our towels, I was already practically in the water. The snack bar, everything, was gone. I felt a little dizzy and disoriented. But there was the familiar turnout of Dana Point to the north, and the smog from Los Angeles that my grandmother used to eye with disgust had disappeared. I didn't wait for more memories to come to me. The beach was gone and we were grown up and my grandparents were gone. I felt it. Time had passed, a lot of time. Under my feet, I could see how much.

"Let's leave," I said. Now Todd seemed energetic as a puppy. "Where do you want to go next?" he said. I didn't want to go anywhere next unless it involved time travel. If the beach hadn't held up, I was pretty sure the houses, schools, and parks would be too changed to recognize. We ventured over to Las Palmas Elementary school, where my brother and I attended and where my mom and grandma had both worked. We got out and poked around. I looked for the trees we'd planted on Arbor Days, anything that might have lasted, but everything had changed. I could feel myself moving on, letting go.

We drove around the town. Todd kept saying, "What else do you want to see? Don't you want to see anything else?" So we drove down to Marquita Beach the beach that is within walking distance of my grandparents' home and where we also spent many summer days but it, too, looked somehow remodeled. I wasn't eager to walk down. My uncle's story of burning all of his high school yearbooks down there after he got out of jail came to mind. He had been arrested at my grandparents' home for being in possession of a half a joint of marijuana and had gone to jail for six months, probably the nadir of my grandmother's life. I thought of the day when I defied her as a young teen by going down to the beach at twilight, feeling so grown up as I sat alone in the cool sand watching the sun set. I was a strong young woman, I thought, in possession of my choices and my future and I knew I was safe. How good it felt to sit there on that beach and know all of that. I can't argue with her now as I look back on that slim fourteen year old, a reclining silhouette in the half dark.

Todd urged me to walk down to what had been Marquita beach. My throat thickened and began to ache. I felt old, so old that I might even be invisible, just an apparition. Looking around I took in the changes: more parking, bigger trees, our old overlook, so built up. I noticed a bench on a new bit of landscaping. I thought it might be a good place to sit and watch the sun set rather than walking down on the beach. As I approached it, I could see that it was a bench that someone had purchased as a memorial for someone. Painted on it were the words, "There is beauty in letting go."

By now the sunset was abnormally beautiful. Pinks, purples, blues, and oranges swirled around us like a Van Gogh, painting:

the buildings, the pavement, everything, the sand and water, were wrapped in a golden glow.

I took off my shoes, sucked in my breath and headed through the little tunnel and over the rocks, just as we kids had always done, and down onto the beach. I felt as though I was being pulled into the sunset. It felt rollicking and celebratory and kind and I kept walking into it, across the glistening sand and into the painted water, trying to both take it into me and disappear into it.

In the waves, I saw a child quietly enjoying herself on a boogie board. I could only see her silhouette. She looked to be about twelve or thirteen. To my right and a bit behind me, a younger child, a boy—maybe about nine, played with a sandcastle. I couldn't help but reflect on my brother and me. What were these two kids doing down here? We had played there just like that so many years ago, my brother always tunneling and building, lost in his own little world, and me, always in the water until my mother and grandmother screamed themselves hoarse calling me in. Silhouetted, as they were, I couldn't see their features. They might as well have been us.

Suddenly, I sensed my grandparents there with me, both of them, in the sunset. I sensed them and they were together, and they were okay. I didn't see them; I felt them. They directed me to the little boy on the beach again. I was thinking about our crazy mixed up family, all of the broken links, the confusion and disconnects, and I heard them, I heard my grandparents say, "All that matters, all that lasts, all that will ever matter, is love. In fact, it is all there is."

CROSSING THE LINE
BY SAVANNAH HARDY

For much of my life, it had been expected that I would follow The Typical Adventist Path. I would attend Southern Adventist University and find a Nice Adventist Boy who would support me while I cared for our Two-or-Three Adventist Children. Any alternative would be like a trip to the moon: It might be fun, but so few people ever did it – why should anyone think I'd be one of those delinquent few?

Of course, once I transferred to a nondenominational Christian school, I saw plenty of other options. But at home my family's Adventist traditions didn't bend for football games or weekend activities or even a play I was performing in that was scheduled for Friday, the start of Sabbath. My adherence to that rule backfired when, out of irritated boredom on the evening of the performance, I riffled through my father's Adventist magazines and discovered an article claiming that Ellen White, the church's long-deceased prophet and the 19th-century source of our biblical interpretation and rules, had plagiarized many of her writings.

It took a while for me to accept that the error described was not a colossal joke; when I did I wondered what else about my religion might not be true. I announced to my family and friends that I was leaving Adventism.

I thought it would be all right: Mom was still Mom, even though we were no longer the same religion. So when I had my first "real" date ever – not a just-friends prom or "Why did he bring his father to the game?" sporting event – with the man I would eventually marry, you'd have thought my choice would make any Christian parent's dream come true: Carson and I had met at our Christian high school and become friends on the Bible Quiz team; when he asked me out after an out-of-state competition, he invited me to go with him to see Mel Gibson's *Passion of the Christ*. But my parents were a little ambivalent, and it wasn't because of the prospect of their little girl watching Jesus torture porn. It was because my family was Seventh-day Adventist (even if I claimed to no longer be) and Carson was not: he was part of the edgy mainstream Christianity that my parents found a bit shocking. In the face of this challenge I was fortunate that my parents knew and liked him as a person.

On the evening of my first date, my mother made sure I was ready with plenty of time to spare. I was only a year into my new life as an ex-Adventist, and I accepted her help as an uncomplicated message of her support and excitement. There was no arguing about my clothes or about Mom's perceived bossiness; my shirt was long-sleeved and high-necked, and I was ready on time.

When Carson arrived, he aced the Mom Checklist: meeting the family, holding the door for me, and (as I told her afterward because she asked) paying for both of us. He aced my Savannah Checklist by asking me, while we weren't quite out of the driveway, if I wanted ice cream after the movie. Of course I did – and of course I spent the whole movie with my awareness split between the gorgeous guy sitting next to me and the increasingly less gorgeous Jim Caviezel getting beaten to a bloody pulp. My inability to summon up the proper sympathy for the suffering savior made me feel a bit guilty – but not much. We were finishing our Friend-Z's when Carson said, "I hope this isn't going too fast, but I was hoping we could date exclusively until you leave for college."

My goal had been simply to get a second date, and here he was, leaving me no time to get insecure. I said yes before he could change his mind.

As we left the Friendly's parking lot, he asked one more thing: "So how will your parents feel about you dating a non-Adventist?"

I'd never been The Rebellious One. Yet this question was the biggest turn-on I'd ever experienced – a thrill that was quickly surpassed when on our second date Carson held my hand, making my whole body feel electrified. I wondered, partly in sincerity and partly to distract myself, if other eighteen-year-olds had to keep themselves from collapsing with desire from intertwined fingers. By then, even if my parents had hated the thought of me driving around town with a non-Adventist heathen, I wouldn't have stopped.

Over the next few weeks, my perspective on intimacy changed as fast as I'd gone through puberty several years earlier, and it was just as confusing and exhilarating. As a devout middle-schooler, I'd been sure that if any boy tried to ask me out, the spiritually correct response would be to punch him in the face. My virtue, however, went untested in this regard; the boys must have sensed my alacrity for face-punching. I'd been exceptionally repressed for years, a Good Adventist Girl, but when Carson and I got together, I knew I was experiencing Needs That Should Only Be Fulfilled within the Context of Marriage.

But my daydreams of violence were long past, and to my delighted shock, Carson *liked* me. The fact that our religious upbringing had resulted in both of us have a similar lack of experience made me feel excitedly comfortable – an intriguing paradox. On our third date he kissed me for the first time: at the beginning of *The Fellowship of the Ring*, as a dead Isildur floated down the river with arrows protruding from his back. We missed almost the entirety of Gollum's appearance in that film.

Carson and I had talked about the physical aspect of our relationship before it began; he didn't want to offend me by kissing me too soon or holding my hand in public if I didn't want to. But after making out with Orc-filled battles raging in the background, I wasn't sure which of the standards I'd been raised with I wanted to keep.

My sex education at religious schools didn't help me sort out what I wanted, especially because I didn't know how sex was even possible. Our sex ed class in high school assured us that we should not have sex before marriage, and insisted we "needn't worry about whether the plumbing works," because God had designed the system. But as a virginal non-mechanic, I was clueless.

Until three months into our relationship, when we went to the beach. I'd bought a new swimsuit for the occasion; we ran into the ocean and dove into one another. About the time I wrapped my other leg around his waist, I was surprised at how much more buoyant the saltwater had made part of Carson – but as I'd heard plenty of times, Boys Were Different.

Eventually I put the random pieces of my sexual knowledge together and realized that penises were not just glorified skin tags. So although I was far from getting my plumber's certification, I finally believed that, yes, the plumbing did indeed work.

I wish I could say that, after that day at the beach, whether it took a month or a year as long as it was definitely on our own timetable, we had sex. I wish I could say we moved on from just making out, a wonderfully vague term suggesting escape and bandits, to hand jobs and blow jobs and other things that sounded fun and had names I couldn't even say. But because my Adventist upbringing taught me the old refrain about boys using love to get sex and girls using sex to get love, which seemed truer because of the saying's crisscross pattern, I didn't expect Carson to give anything.

So we continued making out – in our cars, usually while parked, usually while no police officers or homeless men were around; in the neighborhood park after all the little kids had gone home; and on my bed, which, because I hadn't updated it since I got it thirteen years before, looked like a cupcake made of fabric. We even made out in Carson's church after his family returned from a three-week mission trip to Africa. While the projector ran a PowerPoint about their trip, dedicated to teaching Namibians about the benefits of sexual abstinence, we sat in a middle pew and mashed our mouths together.

Away from church, we threw in a good amount of clothed dry humping – but whenever a shirt came off or a hand went below the belt, the conservative Christian guilt would kick in, for me or for him but usually for both of us. And we would stop. Sometimes we'd do more than stop; we'd vow never to do it again because It Wasn't What God Wanted. Jesus became an unwelcome peeping tom.

So did my mother. Her initial affection for Carson had wavered almost immediately, when Carson brought me home around midnight on a Friday after our second date. Mom stopped me three feet inside the house. "Tell him," she said, "that if he wishes to remain in our good graces, he must get you home in time for Sabbath." I nodded, trying to ignore her suddenly Victorian way of speaking, but her mistrust grew into paranoia: she checked the guest room bed for wrinkles. She would threaten and sometimes carry out a Carson-specific grounding because I was "spending too much time with him" and becoming a different person. "You're always laughing," she complained. She would ask questions about my "new beliefs" and "Sunday worship" in particular. If she found out Carson and I fought, even briefly, she was quick to say she could tell that something was deeply wrong, and maybe I should consider the future of our relationship.

But the issue wasn't really Carson. It was my not being Adventist – and my feeble attempts to wrest control of my life away from my parents, who still believed in the prophet I'd held up to them as a liar. After spending my first college semester a couple hours away, I was back to living at home, trying to repair the rift between my parents and me. But Mom was too far gone to still be Mom. Something in my family had gone very, very wrong, in the sort of way that we hear leads teenagers in need of affection to have sex as a substitute when they otherwise wouldn't.

Indeed, the first time I came close to sleeping with Carson sprang from grief. My parents had just threatened to kick me out. They hadn't even told me face to face; instead, they'd written a letter and left it where I would find it. It wasn't the first time they'd wanted me to leave, nor would it be the last. I drove to Carson's aunt's house, where he was housesitting while she was out of town, and cried as the rain poured down outside. I showed him the letter, and he held me, and I wanted to ask him, perhaps even beg him, to sleep with me. I pictured myself dragging him into one of the bedrooms, doing every physically intimate thing we'd already done and unimaginably more, but we were Good Kids and never left the couch, never followed that imaginary self into a bigger adventure.

Instead, we followed the plan: no sexual intercourse until marriage. It seemed perfectly clear; all we had to do was wait until our wedding night, and Everything Would Be Fine.

But three days before we were married, my nerves ramped up: We were about to Do It. I didn't have any female friends to talk to – trust was too difficult for friendship in my early ex-Adventist years – but from what I'd heard, it would hurt, and I'd had enough pain since my breakup with Adventism to want to avoid any more.

I seriously considered just shoving a condom-wrapped cucumber Up There. A cucumber was a budget-friendly investment in my soon-to-be married bliss, but was it safe to shove produce Up There? And if a condom was needed, where did one buy them? And then would the condom require lube, and with all the lube/produce/body smells, wouldn't that be even grosser than whatever else I didn't know to ask or expect?

So I asked Mom. It was what good girls were supposed to do, and I probably also wanted to assure her that I had been a (relatively) Good Girl. I tried to be casual, hoping she'd give me some secret all women used during their first time to prevent pain, but I knew better than to make any suggestions about vegetables. "I'm not sure about having sex for the first time three days from now," I said. "Is there anything I can do to make it better?"

Her voice grew icicles: "Well, you could have sex *now*." Her face held a look of disappointment that I would even ask such a thing. What was worse than her disappointment was my aloneness; there was no one else to ask.

I tried to be optimistic: Maybe only wedding-night sex was painful and the rest was all bouncy, lube-filled fun! Or maybe it would hurt but still feel good! Still, I doubted God rewarded the abstinent faithful with an evening of kinky sex, even though the churchy standard meant going from virgin to Christian sex goddess in one night.

So, in the three days before the wedding, I bought books with embarrassing titles and pictures of shadowy, muscular bodies so I could study as though for an exam. My bridesmaids had given me a basketful of lube and panties and fancy condoms that I counted on to help. And after the reception, I changed into an over-the-head dress so Carson wouldn't have to break me out of my giant, 50-pound jail of a wedding gown.

My nervousness worsened during our drive to the hotel. This would be Our First Time. It had to be done. And it felt like facing a wall of fire: I hoped I could just run through it and the pain would be over and done with. Carson carried me over the threshold and to a bed strewn with fake rose petals from Target that spelled our shared pet name. We stripped down to our underwear and, after some awkward kissing and touching, tried to get down to business – and, for the entirety of our honeymoon, never Did It.

It was my vagina. The damn thing just wouldn't open properly. As a Christian virgin, I was supposed to be scared of Carson's anatomy – at least, so I'd heard. Now I was afraid of mine. Contrary to what I'd been told, the plumbing was not working. For a month, nothing budged. No matter what position we tried, how much pain I was willing to tolerate, even when I angled myself upside down and face up over the arm of the couch in the hope that perhaps gravity would suddenly increase and help us out, nothing worked. So the next step was to see my gynecologist.

She told me my hymen had completely stretched. Carson, much more concerned about my pain than I was, had been very careful not to break it and strengthen any psychological link between sex and pain. I didn't understand how, with a husband who loved me and was so gentle and patient, I wasn't able to have intercourse.

My doctor told me to go take a bath and have a couple glasses of wine and relax. I'd already tested that folk remedy and found it lacking, and I asked if I should have a stronger intervention. I'd read about dilators and wondered if I should get a set. "You should be fine in a few months if you can just relax," she assured me.

The command to relax did not relax me. Carson and I tried, for three years. It wasn't that I was unwilling to have sex; my vaginal muscles were too tight to permit anything wider than a tampon. Carson became uninterested in the "sex" we *were* able to have. Meanwhile, I became more and more obsessed with being able to have intercourse. As Carson's interest faded, my focus switched to simply keeping what we had.

I didn't think much about what my mother or my Adventist up-bringing had to do with my sexual dysfunction – or I tried not to. I'd been raised with a wariness of modern psychology, so linking the three seemed too obvious and too offensive. To make a claim like that in a society that reveres motherhood and religion, purity and marriage, seemed, in my mind, to require solid proof: peer-reviewed studies, expert witnesses.

Finally, after yet another long day of smiling and acting friend-ly to my acquaintances and pretending nothing was wrong, I broke down crying. I heard myself say, over and over, "I can't live like this anymore." After countless times, it turned into, "I won't live this way anymore."

I found a therapist. Jonathan offered a few sessions of low-cost therapy at a nearby LGBT community center, and our sessions, ironically, were held in their closet. Talking to a man about my troubles Down There was unexpectedly easy. A woman might think I was crazy or stupid for not being able to do something most women, I assumed, found very simple. A man, on the other hand, could be fooled into thinking this was like winning a Strong Man competition.

Several months later, Jonathan convinced me to return to my gynecologist and demand that she prescribe me a set of dilators. I had much more confidence knowing my therapist was backing me up, and I saw her within the month. Her office had a spare set, so I was able to take them home and use them that day.

"Use lots of lube," she recommended. "Start with the medium one, and once you're able to insert it all the way and leave it for thirty seconds, you can graduate to the large one." I appreciated the word *graduate*. I felt I would deserve a cap, gown, and party once I was able to use The Large One.

I examined the medium dilator at home. It was the size and shape of an Adventist veggie hot dog, which are smaller than the regular ones. And it was white, like some kind of corpse penis. I lubed it up and tried it anyway, managing to squeeze in only the tip. Even that was very painful, but I resolved to keep trying since I knew from my research that this method had proven successful on plenty of people with the same problem, even if they were as reluctant to step into the limelight as I was.

I was also reluctant to involve Carson. He told me, over and over, "This is our problem, not just yours. We're on the same team." But I didn't want him to help me insert the dilators; I didn't want him to feel hopeful and crushed all over. So I worked alone.

"It's discouraging," I told Jonathan after a couple weeks of use but no change. "It doesn't budge past the tip. And I feel like I'm fucking that vampire from Twilight."

Jonathan reminded me that plenty of girls would probably like that.

The first time I made progress with the medium dilator, I put it in and pushed as usual, grimacing, and suddenly it slid in. I counted to thirty, grinning and gasping to distract me from the pain.

The large one was not the size of an Adventist hot dog. This was as big as a real hot dog, the kind with actual meat in it. And just like real hot dogs had once been to a vegetarian Good Adventist Girl, it was scary. It was also painful. I put my faith in action and in science.

Inserting The Large One didn't take as long as I'd expected. As with the first, it slid in one day without warning, finally responding to my weeks of pushing and wiggling and cajoling. This time, I didn't care about the pain.

Carson was more doubtful of my progress. I understood why, from his perspective, seeing was believing. By this point, he thought there must be something wrong and unattractive about him for his wife not to have intercourse with him for three years.

A year after I started therapy I'd also started taking ballroom dance lessons. It had helped my confidence and given me a chance to tentatively begin new friendships, and while Carson didn't enjoy it as much as I did, he was very happy for me to have something that gave me hope for change.

But then I made the mistake of telling my mother that sometimes ballroom dancing required a little more physical closeness with your partner – my instructor, when it wasn't Carson – than she was comfortable with. "You should switch instructors," she said. "You should stop dancing if it makes Carson uncomfortable. If anything ever makes your spouse uncomfortable, you should never put it above your marriage."

In later years, I have noticed that her reverence for discomfort extends not just to whatever worries your spouse but whatever worries you as well. My mother tends to retreat from what makes her afraid. I didn't realize this about her until I left the church, but once the initial shock subsided – so much pain! so much betrayal! so many years wasted on veggie meat! I could see my parents' flaws on a less epic and more human scale, as something they learned.

My mother grew up in a far stricter Adventist household than I had. Her Adventist pastor father, before having an affair and leaving my grandmother, had been psychologically and physically abusive. My mother rarely speaks of her father, and I know about the abuse only through her black-sheep sister who refuses to be silent.

But silence, for my mother, must have protected her at times. And as with her ability to keep quiet and pretend nothing is wrong, I imagine my mother's knowledge of her own fear was hard-won. I imagine it was even harder for her to respect herself when she was afraid. After all, what do you have to fear from your father when he is a minister of God?

I imagine her struggling against her own parents, against their legacy of sanctified abuse and repressive religion. I imagine the strength it took to say, *This makes me afraid, and my fear does not make me weak.* I imagine she thought that this ability to screen out everything disturbing would be a strength for her children as well.

But I am not my mother. And her lessons are not my lessons. Blocking out the scary stuff doesn't work for me. My strength lies in welcoming what I fear and handling whatever feelings come.

The dance partner issue was the quietest disagreement I had had with my mother in years. I didn't need to raise my voice, didn't need to insist. I could simply disagree, could be separate from her. I felt I had traveled a vast distance.

That night, when we got in bed and started kissing, Carson was tentative until I reached down for him and hoped we wouldn't have to say anything. For a second, Carson looked confused, his face saying, "Is this it? Is this really it?" He must have sensed the answer because he let me guide him in.

We crossed the line between Not Doing It and Doing It. My patient, loving Non-Adventist Husband and I were really having sex.

In the bathroom on the other side of the door, the contents of my bridesmaids' gift basket gathered dust under the sink: a ribbed condom, a blindfold, some sort of sexy candle you were supposed to use as lube once you'd burned it.

A year later, once I finally got around to spring cleaning, I'd throw away most of it. The condoms had expired, and after that first night, I went back on the pill anyway. But at that moment, without not only our sexual accoutrements but also without Adventism and my need for my parents' approval, we were so astonished and grateful it wouldn't have crossed our minds to be anything less than happy.

⇥ ⇤

WHEN I'M SIXTY-FOUR
BY SUSAN HUTCHINSON

He is the love of my youth, and at sixty-four, with a twinkle in his eye, I can still see traces of the young man I fell in love with at seventeen. After forty-plus years together, he still causes me to double over in belly laughter or blush like a bride. There was always sexual chemistry between us and as a young bride I often wondered, *Does this last after sixty?* with the mutual wrinkling and sagging of skin? As the old Beatles song asks, *"Will you still need me? Will you still feed me, when I'm sixty-four?"* I don't wonder anymore.

At first it was his stop-me-in-my-tracks good looks, but that wasn't enough to hold my attention. I spent my youth watching my parents lovingly serve one another; so blonde hair, blue eyes and a quick smile did not easily fool me. Besides, I was not looking for a boyfriend. Plans for college and a recent encounter with Jesus were on my mind. Still, the attraction was instant and mutual, and from our second date we were together every other night. I was surprised by the strong feelings I felt and began to worry it would fade and I would grow tired of him like I did every other boy. When I mentioned my concern to Mike, he threw back his head with a laugh and said, "You'll never get tired of ME." And he was right.

What most attracted me to Mike was his confidence. He was a scrapper for sure, and I always felt safe with him. He was serious and funny, chivalrous, protective, attentive and tender. At the age of twenty, Mike was a third generation craftsman who had definite goals for his life, things to accomplish and a wild sense of adventure that challenged me. I challenged him as well. "Come to church with me," I'd say, "because if you want to date me you have to come to church." He would oblige on Christmas and Easter. Mike was honest with his doubts about the existence of God and because I was certain of God and His presence in my life, we had many interesting discussions on the subject. Before long, we became engaged and in the planning of our June wedding, we decided on a merger of his Roman Catholic priest and my United Methodist minister. The planning was fraught with complications not only due to the different religions, but also because Mike's parents were in the midst of a divorce.

Originally we picked September 23rd as our date, but in love and anxious to get married to begin our life together, I met Mike in my driveway one night as he was coming to dinner and suggested we move the date up to June.

"Let me think about it," was his reply.

Halfway through dinner with my family, I announced to everyone Mike and I decided to move the date up to June. Poor Mike almost choked on his food, but my Dad, without missing a beat declared, "Well, I say, if you are going to get married, get married!" So, at the age of nineteen (Mike twenty-one), we became man and wife. Too young, you say? I wouldn't change a thing.

As we all soon discover, falling in love is easy. Staying in love is the challenge. I realized early in our marriage how the everyday practicality of living together, sexual intimacy, and communicating well are interwoven. Fierce arguments in the early years, that seem so silly in hindsight over the television, a random comment or feeling misunderstood, are growing pains. One of our biggest fights during the first year of our marriage was over the Mary Tyler Moore Show, which I wanted to watch and he didn't. Mike smacked the antennae off the top of the TV (remember those?) and I stormed out of the apartment for a walk around town. Making up was always as full of the passion that ignited the fight.

It didn't take me long to understand that I have a happier, more agreeable and playful husband when we make love. By giving of myself without holding back, we are intimately communicating our deep love for each other while opening the door for forgiveness and other communication. I realized this was a win/win for both of us. Over the years as I listened to friends share about withholding sexual intimacy out of anger and the decline in their relationships with their husbands, I wondered why they didn't see the connection.

It's the tentative touch across the chasm of the bed after an argument, the reluctant turning over, soft discussion, apology and moving towards each other that brings back the security, which just an hour ago was dangling out of reach. Somehow, early on, I understood the underlying emotional power that existed between us in making love. The fact that men are physically driven and women are emotionally driven is a mystery we will never ravel here on earth. Women want to be understood, cherished and heard. Men want to be satisfied, respected and appreciated. What was God thinking when He came up with this plan?

For us, sexuality involves foreplay, but that doesn't necessarily mean what happens in the bedroom. It's not always about sexy lingerie and Victoria Secret suggestions picked up on the television.

Lacy undies might play a role at times, but to get to that point, sexuality involves the other twenty-three hours of the day. And there is nothing sexier to any woman than a man who woos her – who plays with, cajoles and listens to her. Pays attention to her immediate needs. Wraps his arms around her for a hug for no other reason than a hug, and compliments her. It's kind of like dating continually. I respond in kind, because I know I am the focus of Mike's desire, and I learned that sexuality is complex and many things.

It's me, the uncertain new mother, just home from the hospital with our new baby, watching Mike show me how to diaper our son and cradle him as he did all our babies, in his arms with love. He could always stop their squalling with such patience, walking the floor, patting their backs, giving me a break.

It's his silence, followed by reason when I boil over in emotional, unreasonable anger from the tiredness of raising children, cooking endless dinners and lack of sleep. It's his pitching in to clean up for company because I didn't get to it, or emptying the dishwasher.

It's the dress he bought for me after we moved into our first house and we were broke. He heard me describe it, went to Strawbridge's, bought it, and laid it on our bed with a note on it that read, "Why? Because I love you." I found it there and cried.

The teenage years of sleepless nights and praying together with the comfort of his arms around me knowing we were in this together. Yes, I said praying together. After eight years of marriage, Mike sought a relationship with Jesus. Nothing moved me more than seeing my strong, self-reliant husband bend his knees and bow his head before the Lord.

It's being able to laugh at yourself when you do something stupid, or apologize and admit when you are wrong.

It's painting the living room together, listening to music of past decades, laughing and reminiscing about those years. Or sitting quietly together over a glass of wine, talking about our blessings, past, present and future and being pulled to my feet to sway to a song that comes across the speaker, circling the room wrapped in his arms and the assurance that I am the only one for him and he is the only one for me.

━⟨⊹⟩━

In 2007 Mike and I purchased a beach property for family vacations. We spent the whole first year renovating the house together. Our favorite evenings were spent walking on the beach to the end of the island and back, about a mile. By the summer of 2009, this became a chore for me, as I would walk half the distance, and look up the beach towards The Point only to think how nice it would be to just lie down in the sand. That's when I took note – not only was I tired, but I was losing weight and had constant lower backaches. I chalked my lack of appetite up to severe acid reflux because nothing seemed to agree with me. In August, after gallstones appeared in an ultrasound, I had my gallbladder removed. I will always be thankful for that surgery, because it was the gallbladder surgeon who saw something amiss and pointed me in the right direction. During my gallbladder surgery, a mass was discovered around my right ovary. When I awoke, the surgeon gave me a script to get a pelvic ultrasound and requested the results be sent to my gynecologist. Even so, I was unprepared when my GYN called and insisted I see her immediately.

Two weeks later I underwent surgery for a complete hysterectomy and the removal of three enlarged lymph nodes, one the size of a baseball, pressing against my diaphragm. When I awoke from surgery, it was to the devastating news of Stage IV ovarian cancer. *I have what? How is that possible?* Breast or ovarian cancer history did not run in my family. Where did this come from? The information from the doctors came pouring in and it was a lot to absorb. Treatment options, statistics, clinical trials, second and third opinions, all swirled around in my head, teasing me with possibilities and probable outcomes, not much of it good. I went home to recover under the excellent watchful care of my loving husband and family and friends. I could see the shock on people's faces and knew it related to me because I knew the shock I was feeling. Sadness overwhelmed me in waves. I would think about not growing old with Mike, or see my grandchildren grow up. It was now September and I wondered if I would be here for Christmas? I wasn't worried about my future; my faith in Christ is secure, but the thought of leaving a huge hole in my family and Mike, lost and lonely, caused me enormous grief. Oh, the long and lonely nights, when all I could do was look out the window and weep.

Mike rarely left my side during that time. He would bring me breakfast in bed, carrying it carefully up the stairs on a tray, complete with a rose in a vase. He stood next to me when my sister-in-law Jackie shaved my head as my hair began to fall out from chemotherapy. And over the next six months of baldness, not once for even a nanosecond, did I ever feel less beautiful or desirable in his eyes than before. I had a wig I only wore a few times times for a special occasion, but I was never fully comfortable with it on. I always somehow felt like I was wearing a costume, so instead, I opted for Life Is Good baseball hats in every fashionable color. I own an embroidery machine, and on the back of the hats above the opening I lettered *Jesus Heals*, to give people behind me something to read. Never once did Mike say he preferred me to wear my wig. In fact, he would often rub my head and grin at me and say, "I think you're cute." He always liked my independence, but the awesome thing about my husband is he is so good at recognizing my insecurities and helping me to overcome them. He knew I would wonder if he still found me attractive with a baldhead and multiple surgical scars? Do the lights need to be on or off?

One day during recovery, I walked through the family room with my eyes focused on the wood floor, not on my surroundings, so I didn't see Mike sitting in the wing chair until I heard the slap of a shutting book. I jerked at the sound and saw Mike putting down his Bible. "Susan." He had my attention. He rose from the chair, pointed in my direction, jabbed his finger in the air and asked, "Is our faith in God based on who He is or on what He can do for us?"

Is this a trick question? I wondered as I gazed at my husband in puzzlement. I knew Mike was struggling with my cancer diagnosis and uncertain future. He told me once, quite recently, that he used to think he wanted to be the first to go; to die before me, but has since changed his mind because he wants to spare me that kind of pain. Here we are, both trying to help the other but are uncertain how to proceed. This was new, uncharted territory.

I looked at his face now. Gone was the quick smile, the reason for the crinkly laugh lines around his still blue eyes. What I saw instead was the expectation of an answer. So I gave him one.

"In who He is."

"That's right," he said with conviction, brushing past me with a kiss on the cheek. "It's in who He is."

Left alone in the room, I sank into the sofa, grabbed a pillow and bunched it up against my stomach. I leaned over and buried my face in it, but I could still hear the distant ticking of the seven-day clock on the kitchen wall. Ticking away the minutes of my life.

On the surface, his question was simple, but my deep faith in God was suddenly called into question. My anchor had torn loose with the proclamation made by the doctor of stage IV ovarian cancer, and I was set adrift, swirling about in a vortex of information, decision-making and impending loss. Night after night I lay awake, trying to pray, looking out my bedroom window with tears streaming down my face, but I was stuck. Stalled in inertia. I was longing for health and healing but couldn't formulate a prayer.

There I sat, pondering the question. What is my faith based on? When tragedy strikes, many people lose their faith. How can a benevolent God let bad things happen to them and those they love? Obviously I wanted health and healing, and many people were praying for me, but what if I didn't get the results I wanted? I had to decide. Either I trusted God or I didn't. If my faith is truly based on who He is and not on what He could do for me, than I had to be okay with the outcome no matter what.

I slowly sat up on the sofa, a satisfied smile starting across my face, and peace settled over me like a warm blanket. And I thought about my husband, who from the heart cry of his great faith and love for me caused me to examine mine, and once again, I settled into a time of prayer.

―◁・▷―

When you go through something so traumatic and realize the potential for loss, it causes you to hold more tightly to what is dear. The value goes up exponentially and that is exactly what happened in our house. Through the years, Mike and I enjoyed each other's company first and foremost, but are blessed with many friends. We enjoy time with them, and as our children left the nest we encouraged the other to sometimes take trips; Mike hunting or fishing, me at the beach with girlfriends. We always checked in with each other, but suddenly being apart felt different. Every minute of every day of every week counted. And while we were always in love, a new dimension arose. Always in our marriage through the years, a day never passed without telling each other I love you, but Mike, always the creative one, came up with new ways of expression.

Sitting across the kitchen table from each other having lunch, he says to me, "I love you. I can't believe it's been over forty years and I look at you and I can still see my Susie, the girl I fell in love with. We are so lucky, you know. After all these years we still have that same passion and fire for each other. It hasn't diminished at all, and I mean it," he says. "I can't tell you enough."

I cock my head to the side, look at him and say with a smile, "You are so right." I watch him for several seconds and I could feel the years of history and commitment and deep satisfaction all rolled into those heartbeats.

"I'm just a teenager in love," he says as he goes back to eating his sandwich.

⪻ ⪼

Sometimes he will call me at the beach. "Are you having a nice time down there? Tell me you are having a wonderful time."

"Yes," I reply with a smile. "I am."

"Good. That makes me happy. That's what I'm working for. I think about you having a nice time at the beach and it puts a smile on my face."

That is sexuality. Don't you think that makes me want to run home and be with this man?

⪻ ⪼

He tells me he thinks about how to be a good husband. "You know why? Because you're worth it. As long as we have been married there is still a mystical quality to our relationship. I don't always know what you are thinking and I am still interested in exploring and getting to know you better. You keep me interested."

Of course, that causes me to want to be a better wife. I tell him he is so valuable to me, more valuable than a college degree. I made a good choice all those years ago.

⪻ ⪼

Honestly, I'm not that great. I'm telling the truth. Sometimes it's a mystery to me why he is so enchanted. But then again, as great as he is, nobody is perfect and he can frustrate me like no other. The secret to safeguarding the love between two people is thankfulness. Out of thankfulness comes appreciation. Out of appreciation comes value. Because we hold each other in value, we communicate that in words of affirmation, and it works both ways. "Thank you for working so hard. Thank you for helping me with the groceries. You look nice today. Come and give me a hug." Sexuality is where you feel attractive to your mate and desire is born of this. And it is genuine, not phony because the core is thanksgiving.

⊷ ⊶

The storms of life come for everyone, guaranteed, and often they will rock you. Over the years we built a foundation in our relationship of sexual intimacy, good communication and faith. Of course at nineteen and twenty-one we didn't understand beyond the immediate intensity of our feelings for each other. Life was ahead of us, full of fun and possibility, but I had an excellent example in my parents and Mike took note, maybe because he came from a broken home.

⊷ ⊶

Faith plays a major part of our relationship, because love is a gift and it comes to us through Christ who loves us unconditionally. We are two separate people, both pursuing Christ and as we seek God, we seek each other. As Christians, we belong to God as much as marrying makes us belong to each other. And there is the foundation for unconditional love and delight in each other in our marriage.

Driving home from a Praise and Worship service at church one night, Mike was holding my hand on the console and I was looking out the window. "I was giving thanks to the Lord for you tonight in church," he says.

I turn to look at him. "You were?"

"I kept thinking about how I've been praying about work, needing more work, but I don't need to pray about that. I don't need more work, or anything else because I have you and that's the most important thing to me. God has blessed me with Susan and that's all I need. I don't need anything else, I really don't."

Tears formed in my eyes and I said, "I hope I can live up to that."

His reply, "You already have."

⇥ ⇤

Romance is a big part of sexuality and I have to admit, my husband is a romantic. He remembers every anniversary of every significant event, an area in which I fall way short. His office is on our property, but in a separate building from our house. One day the intercom buzzed in the kitchen, and it was Mike, from his office.

"Happy Anniversary," he says.

I search my memory for what anniversary he might be referring to. It is late September, so it's not my cancer-free anniversary, not our first date anniversary, or even our "first sighting" anniversary, as he likes to call it. I give up.

"What anniversary is it?"

"Our almost-wedding anniversary, September 23rd. Can I take you to lunch?"

I laugh out loud. "Sure," I say.

"You're my girl," he says. "You know, after all these years, you're still my girl."

⇥ ⇤

This morning I woke up with Mike's arm over me. I lay quietly for a minute; thanking God for the miracle of another clear CAT scan, then I rolled over toward him and nestled against his shoulder using a line he has used on me many a morning. "Just think, Mike, we get to spend another whole day together."

I feel him smile. "Will you marry me?"

"Yes", I reply. "Yes. The answer will always be yes."

THE OTHER DANCER
BY KATIE KARNEHM

*"The other dancer has obviously come through
all right, as I have done. She is beautiful,
whole, and free. And she is also me."*

Alice Walker, "Beauty: When the
Other Dancer Is the Self"

When I ran track in high school, we stretched our quadriceps by kicking up our foot back into our hands, hopping around on the standing foot, laughing. When the athletic trainers pointed out we needed to be doing this a little more intentionally, keeping the knees even and pushing our hip forward into the quad, we laughed at them, and then did that, too, eventually without much thought or focus.

But in ballet class, I did these stretches carefully, balanced on the slenderest sole, looking for the last opening in my hips and hamstrings. As a dancer, I learned how to balance on almost nothing while spinning on a toe, then leap into the air. Intense movement coupled with even more intense focus on a spot somewhere in the wings, out the window, on the wall. A spot that kept me balanced and but still moving.

Then I graduated from high school. I kept running. I stopped dancing and started fighting: for higher grades, for faster race times, for the opportunity to matter. For a long time, I fought for a marriage too.

On Christmas Eve, I stood in the middle of the bedroom, trying to breathe as I pulled on a clean shirt. The man I had married let go of my body and stomped over to the other side of the room. As I lifted an earring to my ear, saying *wouldn't this be better late,* he started talking to my quivering pit bull. "Is she being a bitch, Bailey?" he cooed. "Is she a bitch?"

Bailey echoed back a nervous whine. The word didn't surprise me at first. And then, as my heartbeat accelerated, what he had said sunk in. That sharp, pinching word *bitch* was one he'd called me for years, and I had let him. Until now.

Wouldn't you prefer if this was mutual? I asked, scrambling for the other earring, words.

"Honestly," he said, pausing, "I don't give a damn."

And that is when I knew my marriage was probably over.

On Christmas morning, I left my mom's house before anyone else, and went for an icy run. Chunks of snow lingered along the path and my insides felt tight and dull. I had spent most of the night on my mom's couch sending what-do-I-do emails to a friend. He had used the words *emotional abuse* when I described what had happened in my home.

No, I said. *I don't have bruises. He hasn't threatened to kill me or the dogs or himself. It's not that bad.*

"He's been violent with the dogs when you're not there," he said. "And you disappear when he's around."

I wanted to disappear now, in the gray and ice.

After presents and breakfast and fake happiness, my sister and I sprawled on separate couches and watched insipid Christmas movies. The man I had married fixed appliances for my mom and talked about how he believed in egalitarian marriages. I was too depressed to roll my eyes, just thought *bullshit.*

At one point, Caleb, my younger brother came into the room sobbing. "Katie I'm just so sad," he said. Caleb is autistic; Christmas has always been hard for him. None of us know why. "I'm just so sad."

"I know Caleb", I said. When I'd started therapy a month before, I cried through my first few sessions without knowing why. The sky wasn't falling, but it felt like the ground was, and I was leaning out over it on a narrow plank bridge, trying not to look down.

On the car ride home from my mother's house on Christmas night, I leaned my head against the window and pretended to sleep.

I didn't leave then, nor did I have an affair with the male friend who had suggested I was being emotionally abused. I didn't have to; every time I told the man I had married he couldn't call me a bitch, or challenged his actions, he accused me of cheating. He would apologize though, and take it back. Two days after the first forgiveness, he looked through my emails, then sent angry text messages while I drove in a snow storm. He apologized – and then recanted it a few hours later, arguing in circles until the middle of the night. The next morning he whistled as he made me waffles. That afternoon he stalked around the house, so angry and silent that I called his mother to chat about Christmas and invited a friend over to pick up a Christmas gift, hoping that as long as I was connected to people, he wouldn't try to kill me. As my friend left, I wanted to beg her to stay, or for me to go with her, or to tell her in code I was afraid. But I couldn't. I couldn't even look at my phone. I cleaned up piles of paperwork and wrote thank-you cards and planned where I could walk if I had to leave home that night.

A few days later, when he discovered I had password protected my phone and computer, he exploded, demanding to know why. I told him it was because I teach college students, and if I leave technology out they prank me. This was true. That he was snooping on my laptop was more true, but I didn't mention that. For the next week he accused me of being a liar. By the early days of January, the habit had grown weary. Tension, explosion and confrontation, tears and forgiveness, and then marital bliss – briefly. But the length of each cycle was speeding up, like a cyclone gathering momentum over a gray choppy ocean, and moments of blue water were fewer and fewer in between.

One night, I saw the storm coming and decided to tell it *no*. His most recent habit had been to start an argument around midnight, and argue until I backed down or said the magic words that shut the anger off. After the first cyclone of world-shifting angry emotional reasoning, I wished he'd punched me instead. It felt like mind rape.

"Let's talk tomorrow when we're both calm," I said.

"No," he said. "I need you to admit you're a liar."

No.

"You lied to me."

I didn't. Stop yelling at me.

"You're a liar."

I'm done with this conversation.

"No you're not."

I walked away. He kept yelling. In the bathroom, I stuffed a toothbrush and extra clothes into my big purse, and paused for a minute, hyperventilating. *Keep it together.* He kept yelling until I walked down the hall to the guest room. "What are you doing?" he said, standing in my way.

"I'm spending the night in there. And if you don't move, I'm leaving."

He moved aside, and I called our youngest dog into the room with me. I locked the door, then cried, shook, gasped for air for three hours.

In the morning, I held my breath, and left for church.

I grew up in an evangelical world where only quitters and sinners got divorces, and we weren't any of those. Then my parents got a divorce and I discovered the Episcopal church, where even if I did not agree with every theological principle, at least I felt safe and respected. I stayed after the service that morning to ask my priest what to do. He listened to me cry, then said, "I think you need to go somewhere safe for a few days."

Somewhere safe was the spare bedroom at a female colleague's house, and a few days turned into four months. I slept on a floor and lived out of suitcases and boxes. Other friends made me dinner and let me cry and take naps in between classes on their couches. In many ways it felt like my college studying abroad experience again; if I didn't think about the end of a marriage, it was almost an adventure. Friends fed me and I walked everywhere and stalled on the day I'd call a divorce lawyer.

Before I did that, I went home to see my family and spent an afternoon with my grandparents. My grandmother asked questions and fed me, nodding. "I knew something was wrong," she said. "You looked like you were in tears every time you came to visit me." My grandfather said little until I got up to leave. "Should I be concerned about you, little girl?"

"I think I'm doing OK," I said.

"She's just stretching her wings," my grandmother said. "She's about to do big things."

By all accounts, I had stretched my wings years before. I spent most of my twenties overseas. I traveled to England and Scotland for ten days at the end of my sophomore year of college, studied abroad at Oxford for a semester my senior year, went to a one-year Creative Writing master's program in Scotland right after college, and went back to Scotland for a Ph.D. in Creative Writing when I was twenty-five. I'd traveled to most of Western Europe and a few cities in China by the time I was thirty. Every time I went and came back, someone would tell me to travel while I could, because someday soon I'd have a husband and kids and couldn't anymore.

There was little needed to worry. During my Ph.D. program I was also a newlywed. The man I had married came down with severe depression and chronic fatigue – and anger – soon after we married. My travels were always solo. Children were not an option. At the end of the first hard year, he was spending hours in bed. I began ordering yoga DVDs from Amazon, and spent hours learning to balance again on one leg.

In one of the first yoga classes I attended, I learned Dancer, *Natarajasana,* which is like my old quad stretch from track except the hand starts to pull that foot higher until the chest pushes forward and the back bends and the effect resembles a figure skater, not a bored runner waiting for the race to start. The first time I did it, balancing on one leg, my body turned into a teeter-totter, chest dropping dangerously far forward, the pull of my leg bringing me back up, my hips the fulcrum balancing in space.

I thought I was good at this pose until I attended a hot yoga class in Seattle a few years later. In a 105-degree classroom one afternoon, I found myself in Dancer, trying to hang on to my sweaty foot. "*Natarajasana,*" the tall blond man said. "Start to kick up." We obeyed, and the sweat streamed faster down our faces. "Look in the mirror. You should see your foot over your head."

No way. No. No chance. But then, there my foot was.

"Keep breathing," he said. "It ain't no thing. You're just standing on one foot holding your leg in a hot room. You're fine."

Four months after I left the man I had married, I took ten college students to Ireland for a three-week writing class. I had just moved back into my house and was a month away from the divorce being final. I'd started taking antidepressants and saying *no* to friends who'd always gotten a *yes*. I fought with people, badly, for the first time in my life. I could barely write, as if the words that used to walk from my head to the paper had been paralyzed and were now lying by the pool of Bethesda, asking for a miracle.

In Ireland, I took my students for hikes along the cliffs and ice cream by the sea. I went to yoga with a friend and ran a charity 5K with her in the tiny hours of the morning. The organization we ran for was a suicide prevention charity, and we started at 4:30 a.m. so that we would finish as the sun rose on Dublin. Later, I boarded a bus with my students and rode to the Cliffs of Moher and the crashing waves of Galway and the Aran islands. We walked up hills, ran down to meet the water, and took selfies by stone crosses. When I remember Ireland now, it's like a dream of nothing but vivid greens and blues. In real life, Ireland was also grey of the sea, the sky, the buildings. It was the yellow-brown of gorse, and the occasional brown of a tilled field, a piebald horse. But when I think of Ireland, I picture cliffs and blue water, and me following a winding path far above, trying not to look at the rocks under my feet but instead the sea.

On the island of Inishmore, my students and I rode bicycles around the island until we reach the fort of Dun Aengus. One student and I crawled to the edge of the cliff, lying down on our stomachs and peering straight down the cliff face at the water churning azure and navy blue into white. The sun beat on our backs and we howled, laughed because there was no other logical noise to make.

The following year I walked up to the same cliff with a new group of students. When they crawled to the edge to see where the bottom falls out, some laughed. One wept. They all lay there a long, long time, looking over the edge.

Natarajasana: a "glorious heart-opener that asks us to be stable yet at ease, committed yet non-attached, and fully engaged yet at peace. When we remain present to these essential dualities of structure and movement, *natarajasana* invites clear communication with the teacher dancing in our heart."

Mark Stephens

Eight months after I left the man I had married, I spent a Sunday morning in a dark, warm yoga studio in Fort Wayne. This work-shop, entitled Hip Openers and Heart Openers, was the last in a three-day series by an instructor from Arizona. "Hip-openers sta-bilize," he said. "Heart-openers, or backbends, inspire feelings of love and joy. The two work best together." It reminds me now of hiking in Ireland; in order to stand up straight and look far out to sea, or down at the crashing waves, our footing had to be secure. If we could find even a shoe's length of stability on a rocky path, the arm of a hiking companion, or the slim trunk of a tree, the sky was entirely ours.

On that Sunday, the instructor gave us each a strap, telling us to face the wall, then move into *Natarajasana,* the Dancer. As we lifted the foot bound in a strap higher, he guided us to push our chests closer to the wall, to give us a gauge of how deep we were going. Instead of becoming a teeter-totter, my body took the shape of a tulip Instead of fighting to lift my foot higher, everything opened. My heart was a bloom of joy and love. Instead of a fighter, I was a dancer, a universe of motion caught in stillness.

Often in Ireland, the sun is brightest the moment it rises, be-cause it's low enough in the horizon to pierce under the clouds. More gray is coming, maybe, but this moment is a world of light and color, of green and gray, of people and buildings and hills. Enough light to sit at a cliff's edge and gaze out at miles of blue.

Or, perhaps, to stand on one leg, reach back for the other, and push the heart forward. Dancer, like a friendship, or, like a marriage, requires me to find the perfect place to pull backward and forward, until it's no longer pulling or pushing but lifting up in unison.

THE SLIPPERY PATH
BY SOPHIE KERSEY

J on and I were both committed atheists when we set off to take our little boys to church on Christmas Eve of the year 2000. I had grown up with the view that Christians were hypocritical types with delusions which made them feel superior. Jon's background was as secular as mine. Earlier in our relationship, I had gone to live and work in hedonist Hong Kong, and had a wild, adventurous time. Jon had moved into a colleague's house as a lodger during this period. She and her husband were 'happy clappers' who had prayer meetings at which people spoke in tongues and fell to the floor, apparently pole-axed by the Holy Spirit. They prayed fervently for Jon to find the Lord. I really hoped he wouldn't.

Now we lived in Southborough, a small community in Kent. I was working in publishing and Jon was teaching at a Church of England school. Their requirement was for teachers to be "sympathetic to Christian values," which was never a problem. Neither of us objected to faith in others; we just didn't have any ourselves.

We found ourselves surrounded by Christians. Jon's colleagues invited us round for meals at which we seemed to be the only heathens. We could tell that they were gently trying to lead us towards the Christian life, and although we enjoyed their company, we felt we were bound to be a disappointment. They told us all about a family church service they had started. 'It's child-friendly and really communal,' they said. "Why don't you come along?" I felt quite flattered; they must think I was good enough to be a Christian, like them. But why would I go to church? I didn't believe.

But Christingle, a special service on Christmas Eve, was not just for believers; nearly everyone in Southborough went. Carols were sung by candlelight and candy-spiked oranges were given to the children. I had happy memories of carol singing, which had been part of childhood even in my secular school. This community event seemed a good way to while away an hour with a 5 and 6-year old in desperate impatience for our secular Christmas morning. Expecting no more than a respite from the rush of preparations, we headed across the Common to the picturesque Victorian church.

The curate leading the service held a shepherd's crook and said, "This is the closest I'll ever come to being a bishop." He seemed humble and sincere. He called Jesus 'the light of the world', but spoke about him as though this was someone he knew and loved. There was a puppet show that the boys enjoyed. Our Christian friends were there. I knew some of their stories by now and they seemed to be genuine in living out their beliefs. There was that woman who seemed interested in everyone, but never criticized people. A few pews in front were that couple with three children, whose faith had led them to adopt another child.

As I looked round the candlelit church, I felt welcome. *Away in a Manger* rang out in the hush and the air filled with the scent of oranges, sweets and singeing hair. I turned to Jon and found myself saying, 'Shall we bring the boys to that family service?" He looked as though I had suggested visiting the fairies at the bottom of the garden – but it wasn't God I had begun to believe in; it was these people. They were not the holier-than-thou church-goers in their Sunday best who had walked past my childhood home. My family had rather sneered at those people; I was not sneering any more.

Christmas Eve was party night at our house, with friends and neighbours crammed in for hours of festive mayhem. I was exhausted when I finally got to bed, but I found myself strangely alert and couldn't sleep. At some point during the night, an extraordinary feeling came over me. I felt completely loved, and full to overflowing with love to give. I had both the profound certainty of being treasured, and the dynamic need to show others that they were treasured too. I have since called this warmth, inside and out, 'the spiritual equivalent of drinking a hot cup of tea in the bath'. At the time, all I knew was that it was more powerful and all-consuming than the strongest emotion. I became convinced, without being aware of a thought process leading me there, that the feeling had something to do with Jesus. The Jesus from the church service; the one the curate seemed to know. I wanted to jump out of bed, rush into the streets and save all of Southborough with this revelation. Instead, I lay awake into the small hours, trying to work out what it meant.

Because if this feeling was Jesus, that meant he was alive. And if Jesus was alive, then something I had never believed in must be true. God must be real. What was I going to do with this knowledge? I had gone to bed an atheist, and by the morning I had a new, alarming faith.

Christmas came and went in all its noisy fervor, and I kept my experience to myself. I thought through everything I knew about Christianity. When I was a child, an elderly missionary had come to our school to show us a picture of Jesus standing next to a door with no handle. She said he never pushed into people's lives, but if we would only open the door, he would come in. I thought back to my suggestion in the candlelit church that we should take our boys to the family service. There had been no great decision, no dedication of my life to Christ. And yet, the night after that tiny concession, something incredible had flooded in.

But what was I going to tell Jon? When he had talked to me about his religious landlords, I had been scornful. How would he react to this sudden change of heart?

"I've got something to tell you," I said, the day after Boxing Day.

"What?" He looked anxious.

"I've been having... religious feelings," I said. I tried to describe what had happened, and searched his face for signs that he thought I was mad. But what I saw there, strangely, was relief.

"When you said you needed to talk," he said, "I thought you wanted another baby." We burst out laughing at our bizarre situation. Jon said he had been curious about faith since his time with the happy clappers, but had known I didn't approve. Now, we decided, we could explore it together. We agreed that on the first Sunday of the New Year, we would go up to church for the family service, just to see what it was all about.

As we waited for Sunday, my head tried to catch up with what had happened in my heart. Sometimes I was afraid that I would wake up and the faith that had come so suddenly would be gone. Some days, I hoped it would be. It was all too complicated. How could I explain this to my family, who were scathing about religion? And perhaps God being real was not the only explanation for my experience. Perhaps I was losing my mind. That too would explain these out-of-character thoughts and feelings. Yet as we walked around the neighbourhood, I gazed at churches and wished I could go inside and find someone to explain what was happening to me.

When Sunday came, we took the icy brick path across Southborough Common to the church. 'It's the slippery path to righteousness,' Jon joked as we held each other up. We entered the church and a little group of people turned to look. There were the friends who had invited us. Their faces showed wonder and delight, and they opened their arms and hugged us. I have never felt so welcome in my life. As we listened to the music – they had modern worship songs instead of hymns – the words about love and Jesus made me cry. The curate who had held the shepherd's crook was not robed up in formal church attire; but was wearing a fleece against the cold. And the sermon that day was the parable of the lost sheep. It was as though someone had known we were coming, and the words were spoken just for us.

We became regulars. The curate from the Christingle was now the vicar leading the services, and his heartfelt talks resonated with my first experience of faith. Nevertheless, reading the Bible for ourselves left us feeling a bit baffled. We needed someone to explain its teachings, and so we joined a house group. Getting to know the people there and studying the Bible with them helped us to see how faith might be not just a belief but a way of life. Rather than a strict doctrine and a set of rules to obey, it seemed to be about a living relationship with God.

I prayed, and when I asked for answers, ideas entered my mind with a sense of a communication from beyond myself. These moments were like a tiny echo of that feeling of being loved and full of love, which I now believed was the Holy Spirit filling me for the first time.

I believed in God because I felt I had met him and experienced his love. I wanted to know more about the being that had caused such an overwhelming change of heart. I was willing to follow the teachings of the Bible because I was told that it contained his words to his people. This didn't mean that it wasn't difficult at times, or that it all made perfect sense. But when you know and love someone, you trust them. The Bible said that God was our father, and at house group I learned that he was not a remote figure of judgement but a real, loving parent. I had opened the door to him that Christmas Eve, and he had taken my hand. Now I let him lead me.

We were 'outed' to my earthly family when my sister came to me, laughing uproariously, because one of the boys had said we went to church. The family reeled at the revelation that it was true. "I thought Jon might get religion," Mum said, "but I never thought it would happen to you." Both our families struggled when we decided to have the boys baptized.

Friends, too, found it hard to understand.

"It's not as though we've joined a sinister cult,' I said to one. 'It's the Church of England!'

"The Church of England is a sinister cult," he said.

It didn't seem that way to me, although living according to the Bible's teaching was not always easy. I tried to express the new love in my life by not criticising others, and this made it harder to relate to friends with whom I had always enjoyed a good gossip. I tried to negotiate even my most difficult relationships by developing a forgiving attitude. At times this worked and was wonderful; but sometimes I fell flat on my face and felt terrible for failing.

Once, after Jon and I had had a row, I stood in the shower, praying and feeling ashamed of having been so angry. I was enveloped by a great feeling of being cherished and forgiven. It struck me that I would always forgive my children, because my love for them was overwhelming compared to whatever they had done. In answer to my prayer, I felt that God had given me a glimpse of the fatherly nature of his love for me.

Jon and I found our way though all of this together. His faith grew gradually, whereas mine had burst in at full power, but after these different beginnings, we embarked on the journey side by side. At a wedding, I heard the vicar say that a Christian marriage is like a three-stranded cord in which the couple are bound together within the love of God. It would have been a different story,

I thought, if Jon had not been willing to go with my instincts after my initial shock announcement.

He taught Sunday school and I learned prayer ministry, discovering the awesome power of the Holy Spirit to communicate with us and bring us comfort, strength and answers to our questions. Together we led our own house group. Our friends at church became our 'church family,' the people we most relied on when times were tough. When one of our sons, now a young teenager, went through a traumatic illness, our church friends prayed for us, listened to us, did all they could to help our boy and surrounded us with love and support. Our families and non-Christian friends were good to us too, but there was something about seeing faith lived out in kindness and understanding that inspired me. Generous love was at the heart of the God I believed in and the people of faith around me.

Jon became Deputy Head at his primary school. As time went on, he taught less and less, and instead of inspiring children's minds, which he loved and was talented at, his days were filled with data meetings, tasks that he never had time to finish and teachers and management complaining about each other. Everything worried him and he could not seem to relax. By the time he went for help, he was severely depressed. Every day began with crippling anxiety. He took time off work, went on medication and struggled on. He gave up the Deputy Headship and went back to being a class teacher, but then agonised that he had let everyone down.

The man I had known, who had loved me with such relaxed and easy warmth, had disappeared. This Jon was silent, anguished, and emotionally blank. I felt sorry for him, but all the simple joy in our relationship had gone. I felt desperate and alone. As always, our Christian friends held us up. They spent time with Jon, and prayed with me. They never stopped asking how we were and what we needed. They loved Jon too and suffered the pain of his illness along with us.

I struggled with anger and felt terrible for taking it out on Jon. Though the worst crisis had passed, I was frustrated by the glacial pace of change. Eventually, I went to a Christian counsellor. She explained that anger is a natural reaction when something stands in the way of what we want. What I wanted was my husband back, and here in front of me was this person who looked like him, but wasn't. She taught me to understand what he was going through and to rein in my relentless efforts to make him better. I learned to take the pressure off him and allow him time to heal.

We stepped back from many of our church commitments, needing time and space to ourselves. It helped in one way; there were fewer meetings and events we need to organise or attend. However, it also meant we were less involved in the life of the church with its nurturing sense of family. We still went to services and spent time with Christian friends, but we had withdrawn a little from what had always felt like a centre of warmth and light.

Others prayed for us, and we were glad of it. We had not lost our faith, but its energy was low. I did not feel like running round Southborough, spreading God's love as I had on that first night of faith. I needed time to recover, resting in the knowledge that that love was there, even though it didn't feel as though I was hearing from God as I had before.

For nine months, Jon took his medication and underwent counselling, with barely discernible improvement. But then the man I loved came back to me almost overnight. My counsellor had advised me to read up on depression, so I knew that the limbic system in the brain, broken by intense stress, takes a long time to repair. When it begins firing properly again, healing can appear quite sudden. Jon emerged from a tunnel of darkness and was himself again – a wiser, calmer, happier self. He relished being a class teacher and regained his confidence. One day he stood at the front of church and told his story, and it inspired several people listening to go and seek help themselves.

After some time, I felt motivated to be more involved in church again. Jon felt the same. We looked at the small team searching for ways to invite more people into the church family. They were under-staffed and over-burdened. What about all those people in Southborough who still didn't know about the love I had discovered that Christmas Eve? Who would rush out and save them now? Newly inspired, we relaunched ourselves into the Christian life. I began to feel that God was speaking to me again through ideas that came into my mind and through the events and people around me.

When I found faith, I could not resist the dynamic power of the love I had discovered. It filled me up and poured out of me. It was an irresistible force. I would have acted on my faith whether Jon had been willing to join me or not. But I am so grateful to have had him beside me for the journey. We have walked through all of it together, in good times and in bad. It has been the adventure of our lives.

THE CROSS
BY VENESSA M. PERRY

I often say that I grew up in church. But the truth is, that's not entirely true. As a child, I attended the small African Methodist Episcopal Zion (AMEZ) church that was the only Black church in the town. I went fairly regularly and was a part of the youth ministry. My mother took us usually on holidays; Easter and Christmas. My family wasn't especially religious, and as I grew into a teenager and young adult, church and religion never seemed to be much of a priority. When I was in my teens, we moved from a small college town in Massachusetts to Washington, DC. Back then DC was known as the Chocolate City and I was surrounded by God- fearing Black folks who had grown up in church and attended regularly. Black folks living in DC had migrated from the American Bible Belt south, where the church was the foundation of their lives. Although most of my friends my age had grown up in the inner city, they still had a religious foundation which I did not.

My grandmother or my nana as I called her, was a praying woman. I attended church with her when I visited her in Boston and when I lived with her one summer. She gave me my first Bible, *The Good News Bible*. She talked to me a lot about God. I remember her telling me to find a church that believed in the Trinity. I was always a seeker of knowledge and so I read the Bible so that I could understand what she meant by the Trinity. I later learned that the Trinity is God, the Father; Jesus, the son; and the Holy Spirit.

I didn't attend church in college. I was too busy enjoying my new freedom being away from home. In fact, I only recall one person being religious in college. We both loved music and he introduced me to gospel singers Bebe and Cece Winans. I used to play one of their CDs over and over. The music was so powerful, and Cece had an incredible voice that I would often sing along with. I probably attended church on a more regular basis when I was in the military. Sunday was the only day we had a day off. Either we went to church or we had to clean the barracks. Sunday at church was also the only time we got to fraternize with the opposite sex. I chose church.

A young woman who entered the military with me had an amazing singing voice. She sang regularly at chapel, and one day when she sang "His Eye is on the Sparrow" it touched my heart so deeply that I had tears in my eyes. I know now that was the Lord touching me. After that I was on a journey of discovery to understand who this God was, who had touched me in such a profound way. Throughout my young adult years of attending church on and off, I had never felt moved in the way I felt in the chapel that day.

By the time I was in my late twenties, I felt sure I knew enough about God when I met my husband who led me to Christ. When I first met him, I knew it was a sign from the Lord and distinctly remember asking the Lord if this man was who He had for me. He belonged to a church and we attended together. The pastor of his church counseled and then married us in the Baptist tradition.

The members at his church were older and there were few young married couples, so shortly after we got married we left his church to find our own church home. He wasn't the type to visit a bunch of churches, shopping for the perfect fit, and so after we got a few recommendations, we visited Ebenezer AME church.

Now Ebenezer, the beautiful, is the largest church in the denomination. At that time it probably had over twenty thousand members. The congregation was full of young couples like us. It was known for its many ministries, awesome worship and gifted music ministry. But the icing on the cake was the pastors: a dynamic duo, husband-wife team who are truly anointed. We attended maybe twice before my husband decided that this was going to be our church home. I had never actually joined a church before, or been saved, so I had no idea what to expect.

I had been baptized as a baby, but that didn't count as being saved because my parents dedicated me. So on a sunny, warm, Sunday in May, with my hand in his, I followed my husband from the balcony, in front of thousands of people and professed my life to Christ. I was scared, but I was also relieved. After joining the church we attended our New Members classes that taught us about the church, its doctrine, and its ministries. Finally I had a church home and I had that feeling of belonging again deep in my spirit.

My husband and I worshiped and prayed together. But we had not walked with Christ together long enough to withstand the trial that came. Six months into the marriage, my husband went out of town for a weekend and had a fling with a woman he had met on the phone through work. My discovery of the affair was solely by intuition. At every turn the Lord revealed something to me. Beginning with when I picked him up from the airport and he was holding his Bible. My ex wasn't publically religious or spiritual, so seeing him holding the Bible against his chest as I pulled the car into the airport to pick him up was strange, but at the time I didn't think much of it.

The revelation of the affair truly tested my relationship with God. I had never imagined that I'd deal with infidelity, particularly in such a young marriage. As a couple we didn't have anything to hold onto, so I did the only thing I could, I prayed. Even though I felt betrayed, I took my marriage vows very seriously; we had stood at our wedding before God, friends and family and professed our love in good times and bad times, till death do us part. Granted, I didn't think that the bad times would come so early. Up until the infidelity, I had always felt safe and protected by my husband. It was one of the many reasons that I married him. Now, I felt an incredible sense of nakedness because I was no longer safe. My husband, my covering no longer made me feel safe. Who would protect me now that my covering was gone?

To say that first year of marriage was trying would be an understatement. I did everything I could to get passed the betrayal that I felt. We went to church, had counseling with the pastor who married us, had individual and couples counseling for over a year. But the loss of the trust and security that I felt continued even after we moved into our own home after our first wedding anniversary. The first Christmas in our home and the second as a married couple my then-husband bought me a white gold diamond-encrusted cross. When he gave it to me, he told me he bought it because he remembered that I said I needed to feel protected. If he wasn't around he wanted me to know that I would always be protected by the Lord. In the early days, I never took the cross off. As we tried to rebuild our marriage from the infidelity, I thought that if we had a baby that would somehow restore our marriage. We spent tens of thousands of dollars on fertility treatments that only ended in disappointment. I prayed desperately to God so much during that time. I was like Sarah, Abraham's wife. I went to church, went to retreats, bible study anything I could do so that the Lord would bless me with a child. My husband and I always wanted to adopt a child in addition to having our own, so we decided to foster a child

and then to adopt.   But somewhere down the line, I couldn't do
it anymore and I called the agency to tell them we needed to be
on hold for a while. During that time I grew closer to God. He
showed me how to rest in Him, and to let Him lead me. I stopped
trying to be in control of the situation and gave it all to Him. It was
early December a few weeks before Christmas a year later that I
found out I was pregnant. Finally, God had heard me. I kissed the
cross on my neck and thanked Him for blessing me with this gift.
Our excitement was short lived because a day before Christmas
I began to lose my baby. We had plans to spend a few days after
the holiday in New York to celebrate. We'd booked a room at the
W in Times Square, went to see the Lion King and had dinner at
a swanky restaurant that we saw *on Sex in the City*. But that entire
trip, I was very sick. Shortly after the trip to New Year, I lost my
baby.

In the midst of it all I held on tightly to the cross around my
neck. It might seem silly but I felt naked without it and truthfully
I had a fear that if I took it off something else bad would happen.

Later that year, after the loss of our baby, and the strain of a
marriage that had never fully recovered, my husband stepped outside of our marriage again and left me.   I had grown immensely
in Christ, but when my marriage ended I was broken. Anyone who
tells you that there's no such thing as a broken heart has never
experienced one. In my deepest, darkest hour, I lay on the floor
many a day and night, holding my cross, crying out to the Lord
asking him to take the pain of my broken heart away. Until, one
day a few days before Thanksgiving, I was on the phone with my
husband, desperate for him to come home. He refused. So I did
the only thing I knew how to do to get rid of the pain. I swallowed
a few sleeping pills washed down with some vodka and right before
I lost consciousness, I heard a voice that I now know was God saying "No! Not yet." I tried to die that day, and as I watched from
above I looked down at myself on the table while the doctors put a

tube down my throat and charcoal in my stomach. Suffice it to say, they brought me back, but what happened next is another story.

After that near-death experience, I was in church almost every day: services on Sunday, Bible study, young adult Bible study... I needed God to restore my marriage and take away the pain I was feeling. One day at Bible study, I was sitting alone in the back of the church waiting on God to give me a sign of what to do when my pastor called me out and told me to come to the altar. What he told me, has stayed with me for many years. He said, "You've been spared. I know that you're in a desperate situation and it seems like it's never going to end because the pain is so great, but God is not done with you yet." Then he anointed me with oil. I touched the cross on my neck thinking again that God was protecting me. The following year, God carried me through the storm that was my divorce; He told me when it was finally time to let go.

In the twelve years since my marriage ended, I have walked and talked with the Lord. He has opened doors to travel, meet people and experience things that I may not have had the opportunity to do if He had not ended my marriage. Through my brokenness, He blessed me. He showed me that with Him, there is no greater love. People will let you down, but He will always be there to protect me.

I still wear my cross most of the time, and it no longer means my husband's love, but God's. I no longer fear the worst if I take it off; the cross is a symbol of His protection. It is a reminder of His tender, Loving Kindness, His grace and His mercy. My ex-husband brought me to Christ, and when he gave up protecting and keeping me safe I learned that God is a hedge of protection always. I am thankful that through the difficulties of the years, God spared me for such a time as this.

⊨ ⊨

THE DEATH OF CINDERELLA
BY REV NANCY SLABAUGH HART

*C*inderella died today. She would have been forty-five a week from
*Sunday. Her friends remember her as a person who loved animals,
small children and a good story. But she will likely be best remembered by
the world for wearing glass slippers that tended to fall off at unfortunate
moments. Cause of death has not been determined, but authorities suspect
the shock of reaching menopause before happily-ever-after caused a hem-
orrhage of the heart. A private memorial service will be held by friends.
Prince Charming is not expected to attend.*

Once upon a time, long, long ago, my husband and I attended
a religious leaders conference in a far off city. It was our first trip
alone together since our sons had been born and I relished the
opportunity to enjoy some quality time together, and to reconnect
with far-flung friends, even if it was work-related. One of our evenings included a banquet that celebrated the work and ministry
of one of our denomination's leading missional organizations. I
don't remember the menu, or any conversation I may have had

with the people seated to our left and right. It was just one of those banal organizational occasions that came with the territory for a minister's wife, and would normally have passed into mental obscurity by the time coffee was served with dessert. But there was a moment from that evening that has stayed with me, even after all these years.

The program that evening included a slide show detailing the history of the benevolence organization. It had begun over 100 years earlier with a group of lay churchwomen wondering what they could do to serve Christ in the world. They began by simply saving pennies for missions. The work grew. Soon the women were able to support mission projects and missionaries who provided care for women and children in countries around the world. As the story progressed, the focus of the slides began to change. The photos of women disappeared and were replaced with men in suits. I recall thinking "where did all the women go?" As the slides ended, the lights came up. A group of men came forward to recognize an executive in the organization who was about to retire. The usual formalities followed: a history of his stellar service, words of affirmation and the required brass plaque. My attention wandered as speeches of congratulation floated past. I re-engaged about the time the obligatory brass-plated plaque was handed over. It was then that I noticed the woman standing slightly behind the throng of suited men at the podium. She too, was wearing a suit, but hers included a corsage. The master of ceremony seemed to acknowledge her presence at that moment as well. She was introduced as "Mrs. Important Retiree," and the audience was invited to recognize her "not inconsiderable" contributions to her husband's life and ministry. "We all know (chuckle, chuckle), he couldn't have done it without her." Applause. Applause. The banquet ended.

As we adjourned to reassemble in the auditorium, the woman with the corsage persisted in my mind. She had stood unobtrusively behind her husband, quietly smiling. I wondered how she must feel right now. Was she was remembering their life together, perhaps the dreams they had shared so many years ago? Was this the life she had hoped for? Or did she wonder, even as she smiled proudly at her husband's accomplishments what had happened to her own dreams? Did she ever feel, as I sometimes did these days, overlooked, underestimated, invisible?

I felt a shiver. Was this me? Was this my future? Perhaps she felt none of these things. Why did I?

I remembered a moment, only a few short years before, sitting with my husband on a low wall, holding hands as we waited to join the procession for graduation. He was being awarded his Masters of Divinity and I was graduating *magna cum laud* in vocal performance. We had a six week old son, an associate pastor's job waiting for my husband in Missouri and the love we had for each other. This is where it all began. We would be equal partners in this new life using our gifts for the service of Christ and the church. And we could hardly wait.

Somewhere along the way something had happened. Was I a partner? Or was I just the person who made it possible for someone else's dreams to happen. I shook myself mentally.

My life was fine! The moment of panic passed.

We flew home a day or two later, and I felt ridiculous at having such thoughts. I loved my life. I loved my two small sons. My husband's work was important. I was part of that work. I made it possible for him to do the work. There would be time for my own dreams later. I threw myself into caring for our two amazing sons, supporting my husband in his work and ministry, and did all the things I thought were expected of me.

But Cinderella was troubled.

I grew up in a small town west of Portland, Oregon. In my neighborhood, all the dads worked in the city and nearly all the moms stayed at home to raise the children and hold the fabric of society together by being den mothers, room mothers, field trip mothers, PTA moms, taxi kids to scouts, the dentist, dance lessons and in every other practical way make our lives run smoothly. On Saturdays the dads mowed the lawn and watched sports, kids could be dropped off with older siblings to go to the movies, the moms got together for coffee, but on Sunday evenings all of us were in front of the television to watch *Wonderful World of Disney*.

On Sundays I went to Sunday School. My family was not religious. But when a friend invited me to church, I found a sense of belonging and connection I hadn't felt before. The people there were especially kind to a child unaccompanied by adults. I felt truly at home. As a child and youth I was encouraged to use my gifts to serve through music, teaching Vacation Bible School and the other jobs suitable to my gender. Men were the preachers, administrators, communion stewards and ushers and held all the positions of authority in the congregation. It wasn't talked about, it was just the reality.

My image of love and marriage in my growing up years might be said to be two-parts faith and one-part Disney fairytale. Through sermons, youth group and bible study we were taught that God had a perfect plan for each of us. This included marrying someone that God had already chosen. For the boys, this meant that they were expected to be the spiritual leaders of their future households. For we girls the man of our dreams would protect, guide and support us as Christ did the church. It was not hard, therefore, to believe that maybe we were princesses waiting for our prince to come

But, it was the 1960s, and the world was changing. Our stay-at-home mothers were heading back into the work force. Two income families were becoming the norm and at the same time some of our parents (including my own) were filing for divorce. Women in the work force were assumed to be providing supplemental income for their families. It was men who were paid as the primary bread winner. My friends and I were told stories by our mothers and their friends about being undervalued, underpaid – and training young men who would be promoted to be their bosses. Magazines began to speak of the "glass ceiling" cracking – but it did not appear to be happening for anyone we knew.

My friends and I began to talk about what we would do after high school. Most of us planned on trying to go on to college or a technical school or finding a job. But even as the cultural sand was shifting under our feet, most of my friends considered school and work to be something that we would do "until..." In spite of any evidence to the contrary in our own families or neighbors, we held onto the dream of finding that perfect guy, the one God himself had chosen, who would make all our dreams come true.

In my junior year of high school I began dating a boy who went to high school in the city. He seemed sophisticated compared to the boys in my circles. We met through our mutual interest in youth choir and church activities. My girlfriends were envious. He sang, he played guitar, he had his own car – what more could a girl ask for? Adults immediately liked and trusted him. He was a leader at school and in his youth group. He was at ease with public speaking and would sometimes be asked to speak at church on Sundays.

By my senior year, we were engaged. It seemed like my prince had come sooner than I could have imagined. But not long after my High School graduation, the cracks in our happily-ever-after story became too large to ignore.

Perhaps if I had had more confidence in myself, I might have realized sooner that much of his spiritual charisma was pretense. But I was in love. For almost two years I was plunged into an emotional roller coaster between Prince Charming and his Evil Twin. One moment everything was perfect – and in the next he would be verbally and emotionally abusive. I could never be sure which one I would see when he came to pick me up. He had seemed to be everything that God could possibly want for me – liked and respected by everyone I knew. I kept wondering if there was something wrong with me. Finally, it was my fear of giving in to his increasing sexual demands and finding myself an unwed mother that provided me with the courage to break it off I was devastated.

Faux Prince Charming was furious. He continued calling and showing up unexpectedly at work and at the apartment I shared with a friend. One evening he came by when I was alone and refused to leave, so I walked out of the door into the January rain – without a coat, wearing bedroom slippers – and hid at a neighbor's house until I was sure he had left. The next day I called my father in Colorado and asked if I could stay with him for a while.

I quit my job, packed a suitcase and got on a Greyhound bus. As I looked out the window on the long drive from Oregon to Colorado I felt foolish and humiliated. At the ripe old age of nineteen, I was pretty sure that Prince Charming, if he existed, was probably not in the market for someone as confused and undeserving as I. And if God did indeed want the best for me, why had He let this imposter come into my life?

Moving in with my father was a balm to my wounded soul. My Dad and Mom had divorced when I was in junior high school, and after a year or two, Dad accepted a job in Colorado. We hadn't had much time together for several years. I might not have been a princess to my ex-boyfriend, but I was to my Dad. And right then, I needed to know that I was not a failure in the princess department. We enjoyed getting to know each other on a deeper, more adult level. I got a job in downtown Denver and Dad helped me to purchase my first car (It was a Ford Maverick – a pretty basic vehicle but it had a red racing stripe from hood to trunk that made me feel like an adventurer.). On days off, Dad and I would explore some of the wonders of Colorado and eat at interesting restaurants. I found a church home and began to develop friends.

I had lived in Denver for almost a year when my life again shifted directions. At a church camp I was staffing, a professor at a small Bible College back in Oregon had convinced me that his school needed quality students – like me. I wasn't sure he was serious, but he was both persistent and persuasive. My confidence in my own worth and intelligence was still at a low ebb, but I wanted to believe his words were true. By the end of camp, I still had a lot of questions, including "how am I going to pay for this?" But Dr. B's quiet assurance convinced me that God would find a way. My Dad just shook his head and told me to go for it. So, with $500 in my wallet and a used Maverick (avec racing stripe) I headed back to Oregon shortly before school was to begin in the fall.

And somehow, miraculously, things did work out. I felt valued and capable, The school awarded me several scholarships and helped me find jobs. The campus was small the classes interesting and I found friends quickly. The state university was right across the street, and a number of my classmates were simultaneously completing degree programs at the university while minoring in religion and living on the faith-friendly campus.

I had heard for years from my adult mentors at church about the dangers of losing one's faith in the secular world. I knew first hand that being a Christian could mean enduring ridicule by people who called us "Jesus Freaks." So I was just as happy to stay in my safe little two block campus in the shadow of the ominously earthly university, even if some of my friends appeared to be surviving unscathed. If sex, drugs and rock and roll were happening across the street, I was going to remain safely on my side.

Gloria Steinem was not on the reading list for young Christian women at the time, but her views on the role of women were still making an impact on us. And if I wasn't yet a disciple of feminism, neither was I so passive as to accept the dubious recommendations of Marabel Morgan (probably best remembered today for advising women to greet their husbands at the door dressed only in Saran Wrap) to become *The Total Woman*. I was losing faith in the idea that there was "One" person God had in mind for each of us. Maybe what I needed was simply a "Someone" with whom I could share faith, life and love. I began to long for something more than what I saw as a traditional husband/wife relationship. I eventually found a word to describe the kind of marriage I wanted: egalitarian. I wanted an equal partner, not a *paterfamilias.*

As I began to wrestle with the idea of traditional relationships and the role of women in Christian Marriage (whatever that meant), I was also beginning to chafe at some of the unspoken assumptions of an institution that was guiding young people toward a life of Christian service. On the surface, men and women had equal access to all areas of study: religion, music, biblical studies, Christian education. Class size was small, and the instructors and professors were generous with their time and mentoring outside of the classroom. But something felt off kilter, though it was hard to say why.

Eventually I came to the conclusion that, while the young men were being groomed as prospective pastoral material, we women were not. In fact, there seemed to be an unspoken assumption that women were there primarily to find an appropriate husband and become pastor's wives. It was the male students who were given part-time positions as youth pastors in the local churches, the men who were encouraged to apply for scholarships to seminary, and the men who were asked to preach at chapel services. At this point in my life, I had never met a woman pastor, but the idea that smart, capable and articulate women – many of whom had stronger academic and communication skills than our male contemporaries – were not being considered as leaders in the church was distressing. Even the Extemporaneous Speech instructor who seemed delighted with my work, and awarded me the highest marks in his class never suggested a future other than "Christian Education," which was the accepted degree program for women looking for a Christian vocation. It was what I had expected, but something deep within me began to stir with a sense of injustice.

One day while I studied in the library a classmate sat down across from me and asked me to go out with him. He looked familiar, but I had to look up his picture in the school directory before I could put a name to his face. He was a tall, lanky young man, with an open, friendly expression. We began to date, and it wasn't long before I felt certain that he was going to ask me to marry him. It dawned on me that I wasn't at all sure how I felt about it.

By now, I had stopped expecting to meet the "One" or anyone remotely resembling Prince Charming. I was facing a dilemma: if Prince Charming was no longer in the running, how was I supposed to make this decision? I made a list of pros and cons, and found that although the two columns were interesting, they were not that helpful. So, I prayed, consulted my roommate, and ran my discomfort by a pastor friend. I tried to listen for the moving of the Spirit, but the Spirit was unnervingly quiet.

In the fullness of time, not long really, he asked me to marry him. I said yes. It seemed the sensible decision. I felt great affection for him, if not an ungovernable passion, but we were good friends and companions. He was steady and kind and he came from a long line of dedicated church people. I laid aside any qualms and we began to plan for our life together – which included me dropping out of college; he would graduate.

He had been attending school on a ROTC scholarship, so at first, our plans were simply to move to wherever the Air Force sent us. But just weeks before our wedding, the government announced that there was a surplus of officers, and gave ROTC grads the opportunity to resign their commissions without actually serving in the active military. It was clear we could come up with a Plan B.

The most obvious course of action for a young man just graduating from Bible College, was to find a church job. And so, two weeks after our wedding we moved to California. My husband had been offered a position as a Christian Education director in a local church. For him, it was a fallback position. For me, though I couldn't know it at the time, it was a foreshadowing of things to come.

After he'd worked two years in the Christian Education position, the senior pastor of the church encouraged my husband to apply to a seminary. We moved to Texas. While my husband worked on getting a Master of Divinity degree, I went back to school to finish my incomplete undergrad degree. They had no Christian Education options, so I chose to study vocal music. I began to thrive in the academic atmosphere, and my high grades provided scholarship money that helped us buy books. My husband was also thriving. He found that he was very good at theology and philosophy and enjoyed academic success that he had not experienced in undergrad. I missed working in direct connection with a church, but I decided that I would be able to work as a church musician and teacher. At the end of four years of study, we graduated on the same afternoon: he with a Master's of Divinity, me with a Bachelor of Music in Vocal Performance; we with a six-week-old son. And we moved again. It was an exciting time. My husband would be an associate pastor at a church in Kansas City and I would be able to develop into a church and community musician as we raised our son together.

It took longer for me to adjust to our new surroundings than it did my husband. The shift from the stimulation of being a full-time student to a full time mom was a tough one. I loved being with my son, but being at home all day in a small basement apartment in a strange city was isolating and lonely. Gradually things began to get easier. I began to develop relationships within the community that led to performing and teaching gigs. I was also offered a job as a church soloist at a sister church across town. Things were finally beginning to fall together. My husband was growing into his new job, and I was finding my own places to serve and thrive. This left me less visible in the church where my husband served, even though I was still volunteering for various activities. One day I was taken in hand by the senior pastor's wife and taken to task for not fulfilling the congregation's standards for what was expected of a pastor's wife. I was totally blindsided by her criticism. The church did not employ me. How could they expect me to abandon my own path for the sake of my husbands? I developed stress-related migraines and eventually went through therapy and biofeedback. I wanted to support my husband, but I also the need to use my hard-earned education and training. My husband didn't know how to support me, his job was on the line. It was an awkward time, with the senior pastor's wife turning away any time I walked into the building and not allowing our young sons to play together. This continued for months until I forced her to talk to me. I hoped to clear the air, but our relationship remained strained.

After five years, my husband was called to be a church starter in British Columbia. We went to training together and when our second son was 15 months old we moved to Canada. I would be glad to leave all the tensions of the last years behind. Best of all, we were to be partners in this work. We would be living and learning in a different country. But, it was still difficult to leave my friends, colleagues and students that I had grown to love.

We both worked hard at establishing ourselves in our new community. We began with informal meetings in our apartment, eventually moving to a larger space in a day care center. I took care of our children, made connections in the neighborhood, created materials for small groups, baked the communion bread, volunteered in our son's classroom, and tried to stay positive. There was no real cultural support for starting a new congregation, and the stakes were high: we had enough funding for two to three years. We needed to become numerically and financially viable quickly, or the project would fold. My husband worked many hours and felt the weight of responsibility. The weight began to have an impact on our relationship – he became critical and I withdrew into sadness.

It was at about this time that we attended the denominational church conference back in the United States. It was like watching my future pass before my eyes as I watched that silent smiling woman standing just behind her husband on stage.

Almost a year later our regional supervisor came to visit our Canadian congregation. We were advised that without a significant increase in numbers, we could expect the project to be shut down come spring. Our faithful community of twelve hardy souls was just not enough.

But there was one aspect of his visit that offered hope, at least to me. Over coffee one afternoon, he quite seriously asked if I had ever considered going to seminary. He thought I should. My heart leaped at the thought. Maybe this was the time to follow my heart and sense of call.

I sent for seminary catalogs in the hopes of doing that very thing. I pored over each one as it arrived in the mail. And we began the process of closing down our church start project. My husband didn't take too much notice of the catalogs at first. When he did, his words shocked me to the core. It all came down to three points: 1) He didn't want to be a poor seminary student again; 2) He didn't want to move to any of the locations of our denomination's seminaries; and 3) He didn't think I was tough enough to be a pastor, anyway. End of discussion.

After a scant two years, the church-start was discontinued; disheartened, we moved back to the US. My husband accepted a position in a small Wyoming town. It was a lovely little town, but I found it difficult to develop enthusiasm – even hanging pictures, a job I usually relished, seemed pointless. In spite of my malaise, I got to work helping my family adjust, and making connections in the community.

Outwardly, I looked as if I was adjusting well to our new location. But I was soul sick. I began teaching again, and was invited to teach at the local community college, and was hired to direct a church choir at one of our neighbor churches. Slowly, I was able to make friends and find a place for myself, not so much in my husband's church, but in the church in which I was directing the music. I discovered a neighboring monastery where I was able to connect with a spiritual director, and began attending workshops on spirituality that fed my faith and desire to serve. The church in which I worked encouraged me to explore my gifts for ministry—not just my gifts in music.

Even as I began to deepen in my life of faith and feel surer of my call to ministry, I felt belittled and invisible at home. My workshops, community events, and retreats were disparagingly referred to by my husband as "little hobbies." He would often complain about my short-comings in public, several times describing me in sermons as "difficult to live with."

I began to fall ill frequently. After a bout of pneumonia and two major surgeries, I developed mysterious symptoms that my doctors could not track down. I lost weight and felt exhausted much of the time. Eventually my husband accused me of taking food out of the mouths of our children by squandering our finances on doctor's visits. His rage hit me like a fist.

It had been five years since I sent away for seminary catalogs and dreamed of going to graduate school, when my husband casually informed me that he was considering going back to school to acquire a doctor of ministry degree. I was struck silent. How could my partner in life be so oblivious to my own yearning, passions and sense of call?

Cinderella died that night. But the seed of something else was sown in that place of death. "Unless a grain of wheat falls into the earth and dies it remains just a single grain; but if it dies, it bears much fruit…"

Post-script: Divorce is never easy. There are no short-cuts through the pain, disillusion, and guilt. Healing was a long process – for all of us. I applied to seminary, graduating with distinction three years later. It was hard. Very hard. I felt as if I had lost everything to follow God's call. Cinderella was dead, even though she had done the best she could; I learned to let go of her failure. My sons and I discovered a new way of being family, and it was, and is, good. My parishioners call me the Preacher Woman. I profoundly love what I do. Oh, and one more thing: as I grew to be content as a single woman, I learned that my heart had room for love – no, not Prince Charming – but my partner in life and love.

COURTED BY GOD'S LOVE
BY LAWANDA STONE

*"There are days when you need someone who just wants
to be your sunshine and not the air you breathe."*

Robert Brault

I give.
I give a lot of myself to the man I love. My heart, my time, my attention, my service and my devotion. I give so much that it is easy to lose myself.

I have lost myself in relationships with men, and it has taken pain and struggle to find that the more I embrace my relationship with God, the more I love my self. My love for God and myself allows me to recognize and receive authentic love from others – without them, real love could pinch me hard, but I would be numb to it. Thirty years ago, exactly that happened to me.

The idea of love was first infused in me in the Southeast quadrant of Washington, D.C., where I grew up in Vacation Bible School from the small church in my grandparent's neighborhood. Those were the good old days. My grandparents, The Stone's, cultivated a large flower garden on the side of their house with colorful annual and perennial blooms that I could not identify to this day outside of simply being beautiful. Steps away from their back door to the right of the clothes line was a large, thriving vegetable garden most prominently rooted with tomatoes, string beans, and corn on the cob. We ate what they grew – our very own farm to table project in the city.

When my sister and our closest neighborhood friends were dismissed from Vacation Bible School on those summer days, Granny would have perfect lunches waiting for us on the picnic table that overlooked our flowers and G Street, the main road. We giggled while sipping grape soda to wash down the homemade sandwiches—sliced in half or sideways, our choice—and the potato chips that PaPa kept stocked from his frequent trips to the grocery store.

Granny was a stay-at-home mom, occasional substitute teacher, and a recreational piano player. PaPa retired as a serviceman in World War II and a mail man in the nation's capital. They raised five sons plus PaPa's two children from a previous marriage, and supported my mom and stepdad as they raised me and my older sister. I was one of three redheads among their grands, thanks to PaPa who carried the trait. We were a blended family and I was none the wiser. Granny was his second wife, whom PaPa adored and took care of physically, financially, emotionally, spiritually—unconditionally—until the day he moved to Heaven (and afterwards, through his pension). They were married more than 60 years.

I knew what love looked, felt, and behaved like.

I met him while in elementary school in the suburbs of Washington, D.C. We were one year and a grade apart. We were both too shy. Too shy to ever let on about what we were feeling: butterflies. Even as we grew and our friendship crews were the same, we froze. In middle school, our best friends were siblings whose parents kept us full of Shake 'N Bake® chicken and all the rich Hostess cakes that our parents would not think of investing in. By high school, we were the two littlest people who got stuck riding in the very back of their parents' station wagon – the part that faced the curvy roads behind us—as we made our rounds to whatever house party was the one to be at that weekend.

Did he feel butterflies? I was too shy to ask; he was too shy to say.

As the hormones of adolescence turned on fully, I was easily distracted by what resembled love or imitated it. The first guy who had the guts to step to me? Love looked like him. He was cute and he chose me. He was a bad boy, kicked out of his zoned school and led to mine.

Hook, line, and sinker, I gave all of me to him and saved none for myself. I am not saying I gave him my love; what I gave him was my heart, my time, my attention, my service, and my devotion. I put him on a pedestal, granting him first place gold with my family and friends taking silver and bronze, and me standing in the audience of his whims. He gave me lots of attention, cooked for me, and made me feel like the chosen one while his in his possessiveness my little life was under constant surveillance. I went way out of my way to please and spend time with him, so far as to brave frigid temperatures during my roundtrips on the local transit bus, while he kept his car conveniently parked.

I was too nice. He did not deserve it, but I kept giving until the beginning of my freshman year in college when his disdain at my thirst to earn even a college education and the discovery of a Polaroid photo of him coupled up with another woman finally woke me up. That's when I walked away from my first dysfunctional relationship.

After college, I married hastily after a very short courtship a guy who I thought was really the one: I found myself pregnant way too soon. Our attraction to each other at the time, and his desire to do the right thing by his unborn child, led to our two year engagement and a ten year marriage. I did what I had done before: I gave him my heart, my time, my attention, my service, and my devotion. I walked on egg shells to keep the peace in our home. After what I perceived as our smallest of disagreements, his out-of-state family and friends would often ask me out of concern "what's going on there?" As a young professional couple in our early twenties with two small kids, our financial constraints occupied an invisible fifth seat at our small dining room table. In an effort to cause him less stress and prove that I was willing to divulge all of myself with no constraints to help us experience peace, I had my entire paycheck direct-deposited into our joint checking account. While I tried to please him and pour into our two little girls every chance I got, he hit the road to the gym, to study, to drive ten plus hours to his hometown—to do anything—most chances he got. Our young family did not resonate as a priority to me. Haggard, depleted, aging prematurely, and totally unfed by year five, it hit me that he was sowing so much care and attention into himself, doing what he enjoyed like taking great care of his physical appearance and maintaining a healthy social life with friends, that if I was going to get any attention, I needed to turn mine back on myself.

I joined a loving, Bible-based contemporary church in our community with our girls and started finding love of myself by doing what I enjoyed and wanted foremost like ice skating, yoga, and spending time with family, without expecting him to share in my experiences. Although we had already grown apart, seeking spiritual help for the love I needed was my pivot point and the identifiable beginning of our descent.

After ending a ten-year marriage to their biological father, I am a divorced mother of two beautiful girls – a teenager and a tween. And I am the happiest that I have ever been in my life. My relationship choice is rooted, like tulips in my grandparents' garden, in my desire to show my daughters what a loving relationship with self and a significant other looks like. In leading by example, my prayer is that my impressionable girls will choose healthy relationships for themselves as they blossom as ladies.

My past relationship choices bred an unhealthy co-dependency and preoccupation with my mates' behavior. To a large extent I became dependent on a man's approval, which shaped my own self-worth and identity. I allowed the disappointments that I experienced in the past to turn me into an insecure, jealous, and possessive woman who feared what other women could take from me. I also became obsessed with trying to identify possible risks. I did not realize that my own thinking rolled out the red carpet for me to take my own peace and push a good man away.

But those early butterflies. After decades, the butterflies never left. They resurfaced when a Facebook notification said, "You may also know..."

When his face reappeared after two decades, my heart dropped to my lap as if I were above the trees sitting front seat in a rollercoaster headed for a sudden, smooth drop. My hands left the keyboard. First I sighed. Then I called my sister. "Guess who I saw on Facebook!" She and I laughed and wondered what ever happened to his older brother, her beau back in the day.

Unbeknownst to me, when she and I got off the phone, my sister sent the man behind my butterflies a Facebook request. Shortly after, I received a friend request from him. He speaks! Neither of us was now too shy.

And we have not stopped talking since.

I fell in love with him. I love him because he is a sincere man who loves God, cares about people, is grounded in his purpose, and loves me for me. He is honest and handsome. He is the vision of the man for me that has been hovering in my shadows since I had hormones. I love him by giving him what he needs: very simply, a supportive woman who is nice to him. It is not complicated. It also does not hurt that he loves my wide smile, appreciates my quirky style, and makes me feel sexy just for being me. He believes in me and wants the best for me. We connect physically, emotionally, mentally, and spiritually in our reverence for God. We had both longed to be in relationships that helped us grow, rather than being in relationships where we found ourselves focused on helping our partners grow. While neither of us is perfect, this is what we have together.

However, growth did not come naturally for me. I caught myself doing what I had always done: giving him my heart, my time, my attention, my service, and my devotion. I wanted him to be the air that I breathe. God was behind our journey, no doubt, but I did not actively first give God my everything. Thank God, I got tired of driving myself crazy. In order to break my cycle of imbalance, I have had to face my many co-dependent, people-pleasing traits like the desire to do anything to spend time together and learn how to be the other half of a functional, healthy relationship. Having experienced growth, I am more centered than I have ever been in my life. With love, I give each of us space to grow. I support his interests and friendships while cultivating my own. I can enjoy spending time alone. I encourage his growth and I am secure in my own worth. I trust him.

Today, as a 41-year-old African American woman, an unapologetic smiler, a mother, a wordsmith, a daughter, a sister, a friend, a thinker, a helper, and a dreamer my fellowship with God keeps all of my relationships growing. In my romantic relationship, my desire is to love hard while being loved even harder—unafraid of the unknown—while trusting the process of life through my faith in God. At the end of the day, I am being courted by the love of the Lord while in a heartfelt relationship with a God-fearing man.

My goal is to actively give myself the love that God defines in 1 Corinthians 13:4-8. Foremost, I strive to be patient and kind with myself. When it comes to others, I try to combat thoughts of envy, the desire to boast, and the arrogance associated with pride and possessions. I actively try to tap into the true love in me that does not get happy by dishonoring others, does not look for petty opportunities to elevate myself, does not get angry quickly, and does not keep track of personal offenses. As I free myself to experience the serenity that exists in honesty, I also find that love cannot coexist in evil ways. The love that I have for myself can protect me, trust in me, and bestow hope in me. Maintaining this love relationship with myself allows me to love others God's way, which never fails.

My growing relationship with God has swept me off my feet and allowed me to love one of His sons to love me, my girls, my goofiness, my giggle, my forgetfulness, my fetishes, and even my fickleness. More importantly, I love all of this about me. I seek and honor God's voice as He nudges me on when to speak and be silent, pursue and be patient in life. Why? Because it's all about God and I want what He wants for me: 1 Corinthians 13:4-8. Ultimately, I have found that giving God my heart, my time, my attention, my service, and my devotion brings me complete inner joy, unconditional love, balance, and peace.

As I follow God's lead in building my blended family, my beau is my sunshine, not the air I breathe.

━┿━ ┿━

STEADFAST LOVE
BY ROSEMARY ARAMBEL WALCH

In the book of Isaiah, God tells the barren woman, the widow, and the rejected wife that He will take away her shame, humiliation, and disgrace – that *He* will be her husband.

Did you get that?

> " 'Fear not, for you will not be put to shame; and do not feel humiliated, for you will not be disgraced; but you will forget the shame of your youth, and the reproach of your widowhood you will remember no more. For your husband is your Maker, whose name is the LORD of hosts; and your Redeemer is the Holy One of Israel, who is called the God of all the earth. For the LORD has called you, like a wife forsaken and grieved in spirit, even like a wife of one's youth when she is rejected,' says your God."

> (Isaiah 54:4-6)

When my husband left me the day before our twenty-fifth wedding anniversary, I believed I would never feel loved again. Ever. But what I have experienced over the past sixteen years, and what I am still discovering today, is that God's promise to be my husband is something that I can testify to, and is a promise that I will repeat loudly and persistently for all to hear.

As a thirty-something married woman whose husband worked erratic hours, in the pre-divorce years of my marriage, I found comfort in the idea that God could 'fill in for Jim' when I felt lonely. Yes, it was a naive and erroneous understanding of an earnest promise made by a mighty and powerful God to a people whom He loved, but even before I needed a husband, God's words were taking root in my soul. I had a lot to learn. When I found myself facing a future alone, the same passage from Isaiah slammed into my consciousness like a freight train, commanding my attention. As I reasoned through the familiar text of Isaiah 54, logic warred against faith. How could God – Almighty, Omniscient, Creator, Sovereign, Holy, YHWH – be a husband to *me*?

Divergent thoughts whorled around the axis of my faith in God's Word as truth: from "is this some kind of cosmic joke?" to "that's impossible!" to "please God, let this be true." If I was going to believe God's promise I knew I would need a strategy, a toolbox. I needed to know the "how-to."

In Peter's first letter to the followers of Christ who later suffered persecution because of their faith, Peter laid out a strategy that would enable the early believers to be strong through their suffering. Peter instructed them to prepare, to hope, be obedient, and be holy. It was this charge from Peter that gave me the "how-to" that I needed to live boldly with God as my husband:

"Therefore, prepare your minds for action, keep sober in spirit, fix your hope completely on the grace to be brought to you at the revelation of Jesus Christ. As obedient children, do not be conformed to the former lusts…but like the Holy One who called you, be holy yourselves also in all your behavior; because it is written, 'YOU SHALL BE HOLY FOR I AM HOLY.'"

(1 Peter 1:13-16)

Did obedience to accept God's promise to be my husband come easily?

No.

Did the healing of my heart magically appear? Was I a woman distraught and unsure of her future one day, and the next day, a woman transformed into someone consumed with a holy calm with her entire future laid out before her?

A BIG no.

Living out a marriage vow "to love and cherish till death do us part" comes in increments as a couple fords the rivers of life – one day, one joy, one suffering at a time. Similarly, I found that trusting God in this new way, as my husband, developed gradually, sometimes imperceptibly. First, I dipped my toes into the new waters, testing His faithfulness. Then I experienced my trust penetrating deeper into my soul each time God proved His steadfast love for me.

MY MISSION

At the time Jim left our marriage, our daughters were entering some of the most challenging years of a young woman's life. With two daughters in high school and two daughters in college, his leaving the family was life-shattering.

Although numb with pain and struggling with the "whys" of our marriage's demise, in one thing I was resolute: I set my focus on living life in such a way that Jim's desertion would not destroy my daughters' future relationships. That was my greatest fear – that our divorce would damage my girls' view of love and marriage, sabotaging their ability to trust and live out a fulfilling relationship with a mate.

In my mission to live a life that honored God and that would help my daughters, God never left my side. The Lord has manifested His care for me in countless ways during my life – more than I have space to document here. But in the early years after my divorce, there were unmistakable graces that God poured over me that gave me strength and confirmed His unconditional love.

GOD WITH SKIN ON

Migraines were an unfortunate part of my world back then. Headaches came on with such ferocity that I had to lie down, cover my eyes with a cool cloth, and be absolutely still until the pain relented. This is the state I was in late one Saturday evening about two months after my husband left.

Our home had always welcomed unexpected visitors. Aaron, a teenage friend of my daughters and the son of a dear friend, dropped by the house for a visit only to find they had all gone out for the evening. When Aaron saw how desperately sick I was, he stayed with me. I couldn't even hold my head up. This young man took care of me that Saturday evening, getting me cool cloths, softly singing beautiful hymns, and sitting quietly by my side. I tried to make him leave, to go enjoy his Saturday night, but he would not budge from my side.

In that moment, I knew my Heavenly Husband had sent Aaron to my house to be His hands of service and care. God sent me Himself with skin on.

GOD CARES ABOUT THE LITTLE THINGS

In the first year after our divorce, my youngest daughter was one among ten finalists for her high school's Homecoming Queen. The entire student body voted, and the election results were announced on Friday, one week before the big Homecoming game.

I left work to be at the Homecoming assembly, feeling a little anxious for my daughter and her friends. When my daughter's name came over the loudspeaker announcing her as Homecoming Queen, my heart was happy, but at the same time my mind was racing. How in the world was I going to pay for all this? I had six short days to figure it out.

During the drive back to work, I agonized over where the money would come from for the Homecoming gown, the Homecoming Day Parade outfit, and the pre-Homecoming Game reception that, traditionally, the parents of the queen hosted. I prayed. I sought out my Heavenly Husband and, believing He clothed the lilies of the field, I asked Him for help.

By the time I got back to work my head was spinning with a mix of sheer joy for my daughter and inexplicable calm over how I would pay for everything.

And then my Heavenly Husband showed up.

That afternoon two friends, who also happened to be my bosses, called me into the conference room for an unscheduled meeting. After the door was closed, they told me how excited they were for my daughter. They both had kids at the same high school and they loved all four of my daughters, and I knew their joy for my youngest was genuine. These godly men surprised me with several hundred dollars to help me with my daughter's Homecoming expenses! God used the generosity of these men to bless me beyond measure because my Heavenly Husband knew what I needed before I even asked (Matthew 6:8).

GOD'S PERFECT TIMING

Three years into divorced life, I found myself facing formidable financial hardship. I was single, jobless with bills due and no money coming in, and I was hungry. No one knew the severity of my situation – not even my daughters. As the menacing tendrils of doubt coiled around my circumstances, I took my eyes off my Heavenly Husband and found my trust in God faltering.

I wanted to trust my God. After all, He was the One who had carried me through so much. But I was overwhelmed and afraid. It was nearly impossible to see any solution to my problem. Then the words of Isaiah 54 came back to me. I believed that my "Maker, whose name is the Lord of hosts," was still my Redeemer. He would provide.

As is often the case, God's provision for me came in His perfect timing, not mine.

One day in the midst of this trial, I opened my mailbox and found a letter from my nephew. I was beyond thrilled to get this unexpected, out-of-the-blue letter from him! When I opened the envelope, I couldn't believe my eyes. Right there, in my hands, was a check for six hundred dollars! While I was in one state praying for financial deliverance, my nephew, who was a new follower of Christ, was on the opposite side of the country praying and asking God to use him in whatever way God wanted.

The note he enclosed explained that he was sending me the money because God had laid it on his heart to send it to me. When I called him to say thank you, this sweet, young believer was astounded that God had used him to meet my crushing need – a need that only God knew existed.

YAHWEH-JIREH, God-Who-will-provide, used my need to bolster the young faith of a new believer. Nothing – no need, no prayer, no act of obedience to God – is ever wasted.

After the divorce, my loss of physical intimacy with my husband took a backseat to my mission of helping my daughters navigate the pain and disappointment of life without a father around. There was a lot of activity around our house with my daughters in high school sports, church and youth group activities, and the older two in college. I was working full time while also earning my college degree. Life was consuming. When I felt lonely or longed for a man to "do life with," I would dive deeper into God's Word, and aligning myself with Christ, I would concentrate on what I needed to do to help my girls.

And that worked for a while.

Several years later, I hit the proverbial wall. The girls had grown up strong and independent and were emotionally healthy. They loved the Lord. They each graduated college and married great guys who loved them. They loved me and were close with each other. God had been faithful in His roles as a husband to me and as a father to my girls. I was always open to another relationship with a man that wanted marriage. While I waited for that opportunity, I lived single, waiting on God.

The old adage, "The only constant is change," held true as more change entered my life bringing with it new challenges and opportunities to exercise my trust in God. After the company I worked for sold its publication to a new publisher, I changed jobs.

Big change.

The new job required that I move, and at the age of 47, I was living in a new state, away from my friends and family, really living alone for the first time in my life!

Bigger change.

Within the first week after my move, life as I knew it changed forever when evil altered not only our nation's skyline, but also the emotional landscape of our nation and its people. Spending that fateful September 11, 2001 apart from everyone and everything that gave me comfort created a deeper longing for marital love, and the stark reality of my aloneness stunned me.

That was when the iceberg of loneliness hit. Up until then, the iceberg had only revealed its tip, the manageable tip. Beneath the waterline lay a cavernous sense of loneliness and an overwhelming ache for relationship that threatened to sink my ship of faith. Unable to see how God could possibly repair the breach in my heart, I let down my guard, opening a crack in my resolve to trust God fully.

When my strength was anchored wholly in Christ, I possessed supernatural power to withstand the attacks. Isn't that how it goes in all areas of life? With Christ I found power. Without Christ I was weak. I began to wonder if I would ever be loved again. I questioned whether I was even worthy enough for a man to pursue me. I listened to the lie that I was used up and ugly. I believed that somehow I was less of a woman because there was no sex in my life. I wavered in my trust in God as husband. "After all, how can your 'husband' without a body, fulfill your desire for physical intimacy?" I feared that all the years without physical intimacy were somehow killing my libido.

So what do you do when the promise of God seems inadequate for the task?

Pray.

Pray hard and listen. Recognizing that I had to act on the part of God's will that I knew without being paralyzed by the part I didn't yet know, I went back to the Scripture passage in Isaiah that had earlier met my needs and nurtured my soul.

Celibacy is not easy. Can I hear a big *Amen* to that?! Any woman who has ever struggled to rein in her sexual thoughts and desires can attest to that fact. After all, isn't it God who created us as sexual beings? And if God's creation is good, must we deny this part of His creation? Add to that argument the culture in which we live that touts sex outside of marriage as "freedom" and living a celibate life as "imprisonment." Though difficult, a celibate life was necessary in my call to singleness and, I believe, it is important for any unmarried person – whether male or female – and whether the state of singleness is because of widowhood, divorce, or never married.

The choice to be holy in the sexual arena exacts physical and relational costs from the one who is called to live a chaste life. At this point I fear that the phrase, "a chaste life," conjures up a vision of an austere woman, straight-backed with nun-like repose gliding through life with Bible in hand and eyes forever looking toward Heaven.

Uh, no.

For the woman who chooses to be sexually pure while single, the costs are as varied as they are complex. From the physical ache one bears when the desire for intimacy rages inside, to feeling like a fifth wheel in social situations – or worse, being left out of social gatherings – to feeling as though there's a big red "D" branded on your forehead, warning everyone that you are divorced and prowling for a man. Okay, that last example may be a little extreme. But it describes how many single women feel, including me. Often, the cost of purity can be the date you don't go on, the movie you don't watch, the book you choose not to read, or the adjustment you make in relationships.

For example, I love to hug. Physical touch has always been a part of who I am and a part of every hello or greeting. Like icing finishes the cake or sound accompanies crashing waves, a hug completes my hello. Better that I forgo a hug than others misinterpret the gesture. It just went with the new territory.

In the beginning, my choice of celibacy was made as much out of fear as it was obedience. The sexual act is much more than just physical. I feared that giving myself physically to one who is not mine would damage my heart and my sense of self-worth. I saw it happen too many times in my friends' lives as a result of their sexual choices. God used my fear to drive what was at first a choice based on fear, to a decision based on obedience.

The world tells us that satisfying our sexual needs is paramount to happiness and fulfillment. At every turn in this media-driven world we are slammed with advertisements that are sexually oriented, sometimes embarrassingly sexual. Media proclaims that satiating our passions confirms our value and thereby proves our worth. Although my sexual desires are not insignificant, they do not define who I am. As a follower of Christ I know that my own fulfillment as a human is in my faithful relationship to Jesus. An opportunity for human loving relationships is welcome within my faithfulness to God.

I remember, post-divorce, the first time I felt a stirring of desire rush through me. It was a sudden, unexpected sensation and wasn't even prompted by something I was doing. It overpowered me. Call it another shallow and erroneous understanding of how God works, but at the time – and still today – I take those unexpected stirrings as proof that my sexuality is not dead and, if-and-when God provides, I will be married again. In fact, I cannot wait, no let me rephrase that, I *can* wait for God to open my heart to a man of His choosing and of His preparation and in His timing.

So where does "God as Husband" help me in the real world of my singleness? Remember the Isaiah passage? God tells the barren woman, the rejected woman, and the widow that "you will not be put to shame...do not feel humiliated...you will not be disgraced...you will forget the shame of your youth...the reproach of your widowhood you will remember no more." Supposing that it is God's responsibility to fulfill His promise, I deduced that I had a role in how this would play out and I needed to pray, prioritize, and proceed.

PRAY

Pray without ceasing. Seriously. In Paul's first letter to the Thessalonians, praying is second only to "rejoice always," and comes just before "in everything give thanks." As a follower of Christ I don't get to choose what to be thankful for or when to rejoice. I believe the direct relationship between my rejoicing and giving thanks is prayer.

PRIORITIZE

When prioritizing, think eternal.

> "But we have this treasure in earthen vessels, so that the surpassing greatness of the power will be of God and not from ourselves; we are afflicted in every way, but not crushed;

perplexed, but not despairing; persecuted, but not forsaken; struck down, but not destroyed; always carrying about in the body the dying of Jesus, so that the life of Jesus also may be manifested in our body...therefore, we do not lose heart...For momentary, light affliction is producing for us an eternal weight of glory far beyond all comparison, while we look not at the things which are seen, but at the things which are not seen; for the things which are seen are temporal, but the things which are not seen are eternal"

(2 Corinthians 4: 7-10, 16-18).

PROCEED

Embed God's Word in your mind. Study. Memorize. Apply. There are so many verses that instruct, encourage, love, and promise – find those that speak to your heart, and use the promises of God to fortify your resolve to live holy.

WHITE FLESH, BLACK ROBES
BY PRES. MARIA REYNOLDS-WEIR

In the weeks leading up to my husband's ordination as an Orthodox Christian Priest, he had spent an inordinate amount of time shopping for vestments. "Whatever you think, dear," I said when he swiveled his laptop display towards me. Did I like the Romanian gold brocade or the simpler Greek linen? In a dozen years of marriage, he remained the shopper – in our early days he would sling through every t-shirt at Goodwill hunting for the hidden vintage rock-tees – now he asked me to vet his vestment choices. *Would I be able to join him at the seminary's shop to compare off-the-rack sets against the world-wide-mall selections?*

"A sofa gave its life to become one of these," quipped a priest friend. Indeed. When, I wondered, did floral and flashy become fashion for men of God? *Simplify. Simplify,* I thought of Thoreau when we spent another hour contemplating brocades. I might have hollered my preferences, if we could have afforded the fine plain linen, if it had been less the double the price, if I hadn't promised myself that I would never give him fashion advice. He would have to serve the Eucharist in whichever gilded pattern he chose, so let the robes befit the man. Especially since those robes in our culture served to transform him, from rock-n-roller to exotic. Or, depending on who was looking, quaint, or maybe feminized.

Robes, layers of them. The first black robes darkened our doorstep the weeks before we moved east for his studies. The first cassock cost two hundred dollars, came from Ukraine and was six inches too short. His ankles stuck out comically below its hem. I bore responsibility for the gaff, since I ordered it behind his back, a way to affirm his decision to resign his job and give up his music. His seminary mandated the cassock for all students, ordained or not. He wouldn't need vestments unless or until he was ordained. He thought he would be a fine deacon, heading up a para-church ministry. So we remained oblivious to budgeting for all the festal sets: red, blue, gold, white, green, and purple. Within the first year, he sold his short-shrifted cassock to a slighter fellow. A blessed relief to his dignity. In another year, he wore out a second cassock. His beard frayed the piping on the mock collar. The hem tattered. The button loops tore free with tugging and stumbling it took just to get in and out of a car in his dress. He learned to wear it like a woman bearing her wedding gown, a stiff sigh at its inconveniences. But he capitulated to these inconveniences.

What he could not reconcile: when his robes interfered with relationships. It keyed him up in the final minutes of a night. When we lay down together in our bed he reckoned with his robes. Our formation during his studies afforded us plenty of time to see how the robes might separate and bind. When he reached for my hand at an ecumenical conference, we drew double takes. That weekend, we let slide our squeezes of affection. We seemed so much like siblings that others asked, "Are you two together?" Clearly together, but what kind of together? And, in the coming years, would the cloth push us apart? It depended upon his bishop or the parish. What would they expect of him? Would he need to wear his cassock for shopping, on date night, out with the kids?

"The robes are barriers," the monks told seminarian wives. *Even priest monks attract women. Women flirt with priests because they feel heard and safe,* one priest monk told me. So the robes made women feel safe enough to be vulnerable with her priest; then if she inclined herself, a woman might fancy him. Yet because of its exotic quaintness, our husbands could use it to draw public scrutiny, like a veil of attention against welcome advances. Like the minister's black veil, I thought, and the irony did not escape me. That veil drove off even the minister's fiancé.

The nun at the Romanian Monastery of Holy Dormition measured him and helped him settle upon a busy, but masculine brocade of gold gilt crosses. Absent the usual floral flourishes, these Romanian style squares featured periwinkle embroidery. The color blend allowed for double duty as blue and gold vestments to cover most of the festal cycles of the year. He settled on this for fiduciary simplicity. He would need a purple set for Lent and green for other feasts. He could do with three sets instead of five, six or seven sets. She tailored it all for less money and in less time than any other options he had considered. He used the spare change from donations to buy another cassock. Under it, he returned to his life-long uniform: blue jeans and t-shirts. If he could, after seminary, he would wear collars, not dresses. With the rock shirts, he reclaimed his identity. Little did he, nor I, know how I needed him to preserve that identity, the one to whom I had pledged *until death us do part,* back when we were practically kids, at nineteen, repeating the vows my uncle and grandfather recited from their wedding folders, in some white Protestant chapel, waving its steeple like corn silk in the middle of an Indiana field. Because my grandmother, my aunt, my sister were minister's wives, and I knew their lots, I never dreamed I would become a clergyman's wife.

Which is why I held my breath when he first said *seminary.* I was thinking, *I didn't sign up for this.*

"Keep a vacuum by the door, and a kerchief on your head," my grandmother joked. "That way if someone from the parish drops by, you can grab the vacuum and look industrious." Every time, I wondered what happened to instigate that quip. She told me later that in one parish women came over to see if she kept a neat house. Once my aunt found parishioners in her kitchen, going through her cabinets. My uncle changed the locks on the doors after that.

Sometimes my grandfather pawned his watch to feed the family. Sometimes he hitchhiked to another state to get his paycheck. More than once he resigned from a church because he needed to feed his family, or to shield them from some vitriol. In spite of it all, my grandmother joked about it. Okay, I told myself. I can do this. I cried just once in secret. *If it be Your will,* I hummed Leonard Cohen's lyrics. Then I measured his pants length and collar to waist on his dress clothes to order him that first cassock. I packed and prepared with the mantra: I got this. We can do this.

My husband sold his amps and his Rickenbacker to pay for the move. He boxed up his Beatles tees, his Stryper, Screaming Trees, Pearl Jam, Starflyer and Prayer Chain-- old grunge and Christian rock t-shirts. While he played his last year of concerts, he practiced being a man in black. He imitated Johnny Cash. It helped him transition. He wore black dickies and button ups under his cassock the first year of seminary. At home, he wore plain t-shirts with his dickies. Even in a cassock, I drew my breath at his broad shoulders. Still I preferred to admire him in a snug t-shirt. My rebel. My musician man.

My musician-man shifted his gun-metal pupils to the floor and made me glance down at his plaid Chuck Taylors. Nice shoes. Then I gave him the once-over. Nice legs, I noticed. At least what

I could see under the stringy hem of his grungy shorts. His extra-large t-shirt hung so low it covered the fly of his shorts. It had small holes in the knit where the belt buckle caught. He wore a long-sleeved flannel. It was October and chilly, but it hid his well-muscled forearms. He teased me with those much later, after I became his groupie and girlfriend. I enjoyed the sight of him banging out three-chord originals during coffee house shows. I memorized how his eyes shifted from wide pupil chocolate to cara-mel and how I could lay my thumb on the flat bridge of his nose. I replayed them later—a discipline of drinking up his appearance that I practice today. I feast on the laugh lines multiplying around his eyes, the freckles, the expansion of hair across his chest.

"Where are you on God?" I asked my musician-man.

"I don't preach," he said. He hated preachiness in people. I made a note to check that habit of mine. I believed he might make me a better person, just being around him. If he loved God and wanted me, if he would play music, I would write novels and po-etry. We would be social rebels together, and let our Gen-Xers flannel fly.

I caught almost nothing of his flesh in the few months before we married. When we cuddled – blasting one of the tapes he mixed for me, all thudding, screaming Christian bands mingled with Pearl Jam's "Even Flow" and Nirvana's "Come As You Are" – we minded the layers of cloth, at least in a technical sense. I wanted to know him *biblically*. I wanted to more than a peep of the line of hair pointing from his belly button to the Screaming Trees flannel boxers bunching out of his shorts.

On our wedding night, I saw his upper thighs for the first time. They flashed as pure as the bleached cotton of his white boxers. I laid my wrist over his and saw how my skin looked olive against his.

"Do you never tan?" I asked making swirling patterns on his chest with my fingertips. He said he was not the sort to strip off his shirt to mow, but his neck tanned. His biceps tanned. In the summer, they freckled and turned caramel. Blessed assurance, he was all mine.

All mine in his many musician incarnations- from the pleather-and-eye-liner stage to the jeans-and-folk-ditties. All mine under the black. Something in the way he moved defied the need for robes to protect him from flirting women.

Once, shortly after his ordination, my husband forgot the outer layer of his robes—a *riassa*, which is a kind of cassock over the cassock-- He hoped no one would notice if he served Vespers without it, but one of the priest monks noticed.

"Father Joel," admonished Father Gabriel. "It's… it's… it's like you went out there to serve in your underwear."

Except to my husband, it wasn't.

"It's like when Ophelia's preschool teacher asked her to wear shorts under her skirt to cover her underwear," I said when he came in all hang-dog. Having been reproached for the slip up, he tripped up the stairs in his cassock and splayed himself on the bed. Another mental skirmish of seminary. Another silly mind-bender for a priest.

"Coverings for the coverings," I'd muttered. When was a person sufficiently modest? From neck to stockings, my husband was trousered, frocked and trussed. I thought parts of him might never see the sun again. He might disrobed, unbutton, but he and I were losing the ability to unwind.

On our thirteenth anniversary, the archbishop invited us to the Chicago Chancery as his guest. The Chancery is on LaSalle Boulevard, so close to some of Chicago's finest cafés that the food censes the lake air. We crossed the veranda to go to Vespers and took a final squeeze of hands hidden by dusk and the wide folds of his *riassa*. Dinner with wine and cheese after this, we promised ourselves. The inside of the church smelled holy. For once, I did not breathe in the spice and candle smoke and breathe out my tension.

Instead, I counted all the ways we'd break the fast that night. One: our anniversary is on the Eve of the Feast of Transfiguration. – We didn't know when we married that we would become Orthodox Christians and that our wedding day would be a fast.—Two: Not only are fasts for meat, dairy, wine and oil prescribed on that night, but also fasting from marital relations. – We didn't know until our second year of seminary that abstaining from sex during a fast was a church norm. – Three: In the morning, my husband might be asked to serve liturgy. -- Clergy should abstain from Vespers to Eucharist when serving. -- Finally, our room shared a wall with the archbishop's. I fretted about minding our appetites. Maybe wine? At least that and cheese for him? We could hold off on the other demands. When we left Vespers though, my husband was fretting about his frock.

My husband wanted to disrobe for our date. He wanted to celebrate with a pint. He wanted to hold my hand. He wanted a plate of cheese and crackers. Leaving the chancery without the robe or permission to leave without it sat heavily on him. Wearing all night would sit heavier. He dithered.

"I don't think I can wear it out on dates, especially our anniversary. Unless the archbishop mandates it," he said. As if the archbishop would lean out the door and ask why my husband stashed his *riassa* and cassock in the car before we strolled out of the gates.

"Fine. Don't. Make a decision. Don't be divided," I said

"I don't see why I need to wear it while grocery shopping with my kids or taking them to the movies," he said. Now he was arguing with all the ghosts. We stood beside our car, wasting intimacy on this.

"I don't mind. Really. Either way," I said. I minded the cloak of despair the robes represented. They came with all the rules and expectations, spoken, written, implied. Rattling in his head was that line: "It's like you're naked."

As if he could disrobe.

That anniversary, my husband disrobed and we dashed out. We strolled hand-in-hand up LaSalle Boulevard. My husband lifted my fist, tiny and tangled in his to his lips. He put his arm around me. I appreciated that under the black clergy shirt he was all muscle and white. He treated me to dinner – a wine and cheese – in a sidewalk café. We ordered more than one drink. He wore his collared shirt without the tab. When we came back, we hoped to slip up the stairs but the archbishop had guests around a table. They had a bottle of wine, hummus, olives, pita and sweets. He called out "Many years" on the occasion of our anniversary. He smiled as we slipped arm-in-arm up the stairs. The wine and the heat flushed our faces.

I felt so much older during seminary. With the archbishop's blessing my husband made his final decision to hang up his cassock unless he was serving. He puts on tabbed shirts and slacks about the town. On date nights he wears his rock-n-roll getup.

"It's been harder than I thought," I realized aloud. What came between us was not cloth. It was all the cloth represents and what clings to it.

Most Fridays, after we've snuck out for some alone time, we're too hosed to do more than end the night with a game, a film, a glass or a mug of something. The Saturday morning slot, where we once took a date to liturgy, has become one of the quiet reprieves from the beck and call of ministering. Sometimes, while I draw curly-cues on his chest during a Saturday morning snuggle, I think of the young parents in our parish who are feeding their kids breakfast. Some older couple is milking goats or gardening. I spend a long time tracing the lines, the gray hairs, the new moles on his white arms, his white skin, and lean in to drink him with all my senses. He smells like he's been soaked in a bit of spice, a hint of incense.

ABOUT THE AUTHOR

Venessa Marie Perry draws from her experiences as the chief relationship strategist and founder of LoveWrite, which helps people understand ways to experience love.

Perry has spent her career working with individuals and couples in relationships and encouraging them to find healthy, positive ways of working through issues. She focuses on pragmatism and realism over theory and pulls from her background in psychology to advise her clients.

As Perry says, "Love is an action, not an emotion." Her writing is deeply influenced by this idea. For more information, visit www.thelovewrite.com.

www.ingramcontent.com/pod-product-compliance
Lightning Source LLC
LaVergne TN
LVHW091306080426
835510LV00007B/388